THE CULT
FILES

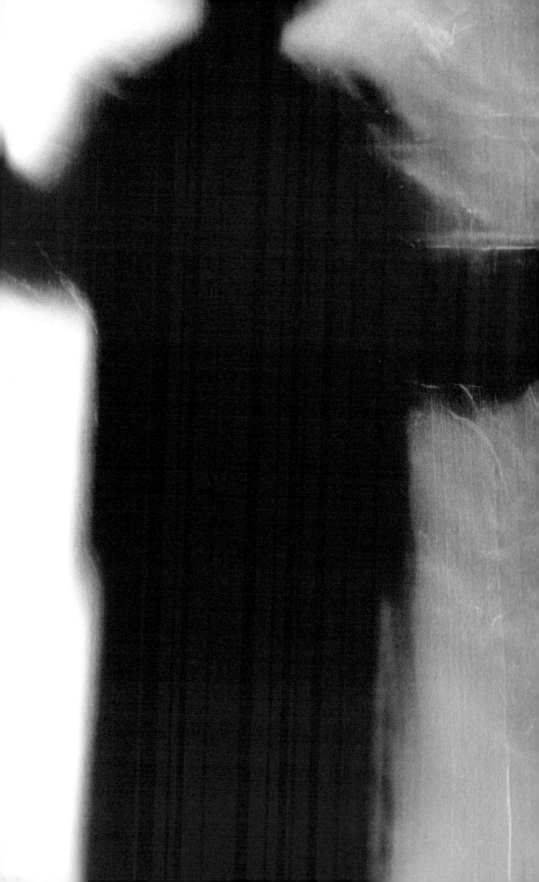

THE CULT

FILES

TRUE STORIES FROM
THE EXTREME EDGES
OF RELIGIOUS BELIEF

CHRIS MIKUL

METRO BOOKS
NEW YORK

CONTENTS

IN+R⊕DUC+I⊕N

THIS IS A BOOK ABOUT THE EXTREMES OF RELIGIOUS BELIEF. Some of the behavior recounted in the following pages will strike most people as bizarre, incomprehensible, even insane. How is it that seemingly rational individuals can hand over their lives, and sometimes the lives of their children, to a cult leader whose overriding motivation seems to be maintaining total control over them, whatever the cost? When this question is asked, the answer usually given consists of one word—brainwashing. But what is brainwashing, and does it explain the cult phenomenon?

Before answering these important questions, we need to look at what people actually mean by the word 'cult.'

All new spiritual movements, whether they are offshoots of established religions or, as is much less often the case, incorporate genuinely new beliefs, are treated with suspicion by mainstream society. The word 'cult' was originally a term used to describe a group with a single object of worship (the cult of the Virgin Mary, for example, or the Thuggee, who worshipped Kali). It can also be applied to the first stage of a spiritual movement, when a charismatic leader draws together a few followers and begins to formulate a doctrine. In this sense, all religions began as cults. During the nineteenth century, communities like Oneida, founded by the American advocate of 'free love,' John Humphrey Noyes, were treated with some suspicion by their neighbors, but society as a whole saw them as harmless eccentrics. As the twentieth century wore on, however, the term 'cult' began to take on more pejorative overtones, until concern about new religious groups became a full-blown moral panic in the 1970s.

The question of what distinguishes a cult from a religion is a vexed one. It is not simply a matter of belief, for as strange as the teachings of some cult leaders may seem to most people, there are ultimately no objective proofs for any religious belief. To put it bluntly, one person's cult is another's religion. This book tells the stories of some of the most notorious cults, the ones that made headlines when they descended into mayhem, murder and mass suicide, but it should be remembered that these represent only a tiny minority of the non-mainstream religious groups that have existed and continue to exist around the world. According to the Japanese government's Agency for Cultural Affairs, there were 182,000 religious corporations registered in Japan in 2007. A fair few of these would probably be considered by most people to be cults. Yet who has heard of any Japanese cult other than Aum Shinrikyo, perpetrators of the notorious gas attacks on the Tokyo subway system?

The demonization of certain religious movements that took place during the 1960s and '70s also needs to be seen in the context of the social upheavals of the period, including the rise of the counterculture, the sexual revolution, racial tensions and the explosion in recreational drug use. For many of the older generation, of course, these developments were deplorable and threatening. Much of the antagonism directed at three of the most visible new religious movements, the Unification Church (the Moonies), the Children of God and the Hare Krishnas, undoubtedly stemmed from the fact that they actively targeted young people, and the media inflamed the situation by exaggerating their numbers and influence. Ironically, many who joined the Moonies, the Krishnas, *et al*. during these years were also reacting against the counterculture, and in particular its glorification of hedonism and rejection of individual responsibility. They saw that these movements were trying to fundamentally change the way that human beings relate to each other, albeit in very different ways. This blending of the religious and the revolutionary is very different to the attitude of mainstream religions, which will often criticize the dominant culture, but are generally content to live within it.

Because many people found it inconceivable that their children or relatives had made a rational decision to join the groups labeled as cults by the media, the idea grew that cults had developed new and insidious methods for luring and holding their victims—in short, that they brainwashed them.

The term 'brainwashing' was coined by a journalist and CIA employee, Edward Hunter, in 1950. Hunter used it to describe the 'thought-reform' programs that were a feature of Mao's China, but the term gained a much wider currency during the Korean War. The Korean communists sought to reeducate the enemy soldiers they captured, with techniques typically involving isolation, food and sleep deprivation, interrogation and torture, while signs of a change in attitude garnered rewards and praise. The upshot was that a number of American POWs came forward to denounce their government and embrace communism.

One of the problems with trying to impose this model on religious movements is that two factors in it, perhaps the key factors—imprisonment and violence—are generally absent. (Of the groups considered in this book, perhaps only Aum Shinrikyo, the latter days of Jonestown, and the crazed Roch Thériault's Ant Hill Kids really fit the bill.) And in any case, it seems that the 'brainwashing' practiced by the Korean communists was decidedly not effective. In *The Mind Manipulators*, Alan W. Scheflin and Edward M. Opton note that, of 3500 Americans taken prisoner during the war, only fifty were made to utter pro-communist statements, and only ten of these ultimately remained in North Korea after the war ended.

The strongest argument against the idea that cults brainwash people is the very large turnover in membership that they typically experience. Yet brainwashing is a compelling idea, and an oddly comforting one to people trying to understand why their loved ones have joined a group that they see as crazy. It became the justification for the controversial practice of 'deprogramming,' where cult members were kidnapped and held against their will until they renounced (or pretended to renounce) their beliefs.

Brainwashing is, I believe, an emotive term for a process that is not at all mysterious or unusual. Any person who joins a group will begin to take on its attributes and identify with its goals, whether it is a company, a sporting team, a political party or a country. It is this natural tendency, essentially a tribal instinct hardwired into us all, that cult leaders exploit, and the people who decide to follow them are often particularly ripe for such exploitation. They are usually young, perhaps already estranged from their parents, dissatisfied with their lives and with society. Cult leaders often make the process of group identification more intense by giving their followers new names and forbidding them to contact people outside the group, including their families. Of course, the stakes are high here—an individual's perceived salvation. The fact that a cult's ideas may seem completely outlandish to outsiders actually aids the process, for once these ideas are accepted by the follower, they form another barrier against the world outside. Nevertheless, academic studies of cults since the 1970s consistently show that most people who join them do not stay for long. (A 1994 study by Chambers, Langone, Dole and Grice found the average length of stay was 6.7 years.)

The terrible end of Jim Jones and the Peoples Temple in 1978 cemented in the public mind the image of the evil cult leader enticing deluded followers to their deaths. By the time the siege of Waco started fifteen years later, everyone from the government and police officials handling the situation, down to ordinary people watching news coverage on TV, had the template of Jonestown in their heads. When it came, the conflagration that ended the siege and took the lives of some eighty men, women and children seemed inevitable.

As the ashes cooled, however, it became clear that the story of Waco was not nearly as straightforward as the media had made out. Many of those killed had been members of the Branch Davidian sect for generations, long before Vernon Howell, the future David Koresh, had joined. It seems clear that Koresh was sincere in his beliefs, and the FBI's version of events—that the Davidians planned and carried out a mass suicide by setting fire to their compound—has been comprehensively taken apart.

Since the late 1970s, sociologists have been attempting to bring some objectivity to the debate on cults. They rightly criticize the scaremongering that typifies media coverage of them, and reject the word itself, replacing it with the more neutral term 'new religious movement' (NRM). There is much to commend in this approach. It must be said, though, that the result has been a number of books and articles about various NRMs which are thoroughly researched, full of useful data and often insightful, yet which almost wilfully ignore obviously avaricious, controlling, self-aggrandizing and criminal behavior on the part of some of their leaders. In this book, I've tried to strike a balance, sticking to the facts, reserving judgment, but omitting none of the lurid details that are an integral part of these stories.

What ultimately separates the groups routinely labeled 'cults' from more established religions is the level of commitment they seek (over and above embracing an unusual set of doctrines). This can range from a financial commitment—the expectation that members give 10 percent, or 100 percent, of their income to it—to the demand that they give up their lives for it. Cults provide a window into the extraordinary variety of religious beliefs, and the lengths that people may go to cling to them, whatever the consequences to themselves and others. They are also, without exception, fascinating stories, full of larger-than-life characters and elaborate mythologies, where incredible depravity can coexist with the highest of human aspirations.

11

The cult of
S+RANGLERS

Thuggee

(Began c. fourteenth century—
suppressed late 1830s)

It is a maxim with these assassins that 'Dead men tell no tales,' and upon this maxim they invariably act.

William Sleeman

BY THE MIDDLE OF THE EIGHTEENTH CENTURY, the once mighty Mongol Empire, an Islamic dynasty which at the height of its power had ruled almost the entire Indian subcontinent, was in steep decline. Increasingly corrupt and unpopular with the majority Hindu population, its army faced revolts on several fronts. A number of regions declared their independence, while the Hindu rulers called the Maratha, who controlled much of central India, grew increasingly aggressive.

This political chaos threatened the vast profits of the British East India Company, which had been granted a monopoly on trade with India by the British government at the beginning of the seventeenth century. Over the years, the Company had obtained control of some Indian territory, particularly along the east coast, and now greatly increased its military capacity by importing troops from Britain and recruiting natives (known as sepoys). In 1757, a combined force of 3000 men commanded by Robert Clive defeated the Nawab of Bengal's forces at the Battle of Plassey. The *India Act* of 1784 transformed the Company into an arm of the British government, by which time it had spread its authority over most of northern India. In 1803, the governor-general of British India, Richard Wellesley (brother of the future Duke of Wellington), attacked the two main Maratha leaders, defeated their armies and forced them into an alliance with the British.

The British government was reluctant to expend the vast resources required to bring all of India under its dominion, and the center of the country, much of it devastated by decades of war, remained chaotic and virtually lawless. Many former soldiers and others who had lost their livelihoods turned to robbery. Indian society had long been plagued by gangs of robbers, called dacoits, who targeted travelers, the houses of the wealthy, and sometimes entire villages. They were ruthless and would kill if necessary. In their own villages, they provided much-needed income, and were often treated as heroes.

As the Company's administrators struggled to deal with the rise in crime, they noticed a curious development. It seemed that a new class of robbers had appeared, who used strangling as their preferred method of killing, and, unlike the dacoits, *always* murdered their victims.

In 1807, a British magistrate named William Wright, based near Madras (now Chennai) in southern India, became one of the first Company men to deal directly with this new phenomenon. A group of stranglers was arrested by chance, and some confessed to involvement in murders. Wright began to build up a picture of their activities. He noted that the gangs, which were numerous and traveled widely through the plains of southern India, had their own slang and very specific customs. They generally used lengths of cloth to strangle their victims, who were invariably travelers, and cut the bodies open so they would not bloat and draw attention to themselves after they were buried.

He also noted one very unusual practice of the stranglers. After choosing their victims, they would gain their trust and travel some distance with them before murdering them.

THE B⊕DIES IN THE WELLS

In 1808, another British magistrate, Thomas Perry, arrived in the town of Etawah, in northern India, and soon found that it was the center of a bewildering crime wave. Almost once a week, corpses were turning up in the wells lining the roads leading into it. They were always naked, showed signs of strangulation, and had their bellies cut open. As no one from the area came forward to identify them, they were clearly travelers who had been robbed and murdered. But with no witnesses to the crimes, Perry was powerless to arrest anyone. He was a methodical man, however, and determined to find out what was going on.

Perry would have found William Wright's reports invaluable. The East India Company was divided into three 'presidencies', however, and there was little sharing of information between them. Etawah was part of the Bengal Presidency, and Perry had no way of reading about the discoveries made by his counterpart in Madras.

Perry had a checkpoint set up on one of the roads where many bodies had been found, and posted a large reward. Eighteen months later, after receiving a tip-off, police in a nearby village arrested eight men. Under interrogation, one of them, Gholam Hossyn, gave his occupation as 'Thug.'

Hossyn eventually admitted to having taken part in more than ninety murders over three years. Others confessed, with one man claiming to have personally strangled forty-five victims. Perry was astonished to realize that hundreds of Thugs in various gangs were operating around Etawah. Using the information he had obtained, Perry's men arrested some seventy gang members. Others fled the area, many crossing the border into Maratha-controlled territory. Those who had been captured were sent to Bengal for trial, but here the difficulty of prosecuting Thugs became apparent. Indian law at the time required that a murdered person's family make a formal complaint before a murderer could be convicted. As the Etawah Thugs' victims were unknown, the Thugs were acquitted.

In 1812, Perry ordered a party of British and sepoy troops, under the command of Nathaniel Halhed, to travel to company-controlled Sindouse, where gangs of Thugs were reported to be operating under the protection of a landowner named Laljee. After spending several weeks attempting to subdue and disarm the population, Halhed and some of his men were ambushed and an officer was killed. Reinforcements were sent in and Laljee was pursued across the Maratha border to the village of Murnae, long a Thug stronghold. Finding it deserted, they torched it.

Perry's campaign cleared the area around Etawah of stranglers, and the number of bodies found in its wells decreased dramatically. The Company had neither the resources nor the inclination to mount a serious campaign against the Thugs, however, especially those outside the territories it controlled. Some officials remained sceptical about the existence of Thugs, finding it hard to believe that such well-organized and deadly gangs could have been secretly operating in their areas. Others became aware of the threat posed to the Company by the Thugs, who often targeted its sepoys as they traveled home on leave. Gradually, information was gathered and disseminated across the Company, and warnings were issued to its men.

17

WORSHIPPERS OF KALI

The word 'Thug' comes from the Hindi *thag*, which may in turn derive from the Sanskrit word *sthag*, meaning 'to conceal.' While the earliest known reference to Thugs comes from the fourteenth century, many now believe that the gangs in the form that Perry found them had existed for 150 to 200 years. The oral traditions of some Thugs traced their ancestry back to seven families who lived in Delhi during the reign of the Mongol emperor Akbar the Great, in the latter half of the seventeenth century. According to this tradition, the families fell out with the emperor and were then dispersed across the subcontinent.

The Thugs (interestingly, even the Muslims among them) worshipped the Hindu deity Kali, the goddess of death and destruction (but also of creation). They believed that Kali directed their actions, and that they would not be punished after death for them. They were constantly on the lookout for omens from Kali, usually in the behavior of birds and animals (the hooting of an owl during the day, for example, would generally cause the gang's leader, or *jemader*, to abandon an operation).

Before setting out on an expedition, Thugs carried out an elaborate ritual with the pickax that would later be used to dig the graves of their victims. The pickax head was washed in various substances, marked and passed seven times through a fire as incantations were said over it. It was then buried pointing in the direction in which the gang planned to head (Kali, it was believed, could point the pickax in a more auspicious direction during the night). Alternatively, some Thugs would place the pickax in a well during the night. Many later swore that they had seen pickaxes rise out of the wells the following morning of their own accord.

The Thugs considered their profession a holy and honorable one, entirely different to that of the run-of-the-mill dacoits, and their operations were governed by many rules. In theory, they were prohibited from killing women, foreigners, members of some castes, lepers, cripples, goldsmiths, potters, oil vendors, elephant drivers and a host of others. In practice, they sometimes ignored these rules, especially the prohibition on killing women.

Thugs generally traveled in gangs of between ten and forty men (although gangs of 200 or more were not unknown). Occasionally gangs teamed up to pursue a particularly rich prize. Some gang members were hereditary Thugs whose families had been involved in thugging for generations. Others, usually driven by poverty, might take up thugging for a year or two, then return to their normal occupations. While a few gangs were relatively stable, others might be formed by a *jemader* for a single expedition lasting a month or so. Thugs could come from any of the Hindu castes, and about a third of them were Muslims.

The Thugs developed a fiendishly efficient system for selecting, killing and disposing of their victims. Having identified a target, generally a small band of travelers who looked as though they had something worth stealing, the best-dressed and most charming member of the gang, known as the inveigler, introduced himself and gained their trust. Thugs often posed as merchants or soldiers, and varied their identities to better ingratiate themselves (a Hindu might pose as a Muslim, for example, if the intended victim was Muslim). The inveigler explained that he and his companions were traveling in the same direction, and suggested that they team up. Many travelers, hoping for safety in numbers, agreed. The Thugs then took to the road with their victims. Along the way, they would be joined by other members of the gang, until the victims were heavily outnumbered. It was sometimes several days before a suitable opportunity and location became available for their murder (some favored killing spots, called *beles*, were used many times). Killings usually took place in the evening, when the victims were weary from the day's travel.

Thugs used various methods to despatch their victims, including a noose and occasionally poison, but by the beginning of the nineteenth century the most common method was strangulation using an easily concealed length of cloth with a knot tied at one end to provide a better grip, called a *ruhmal*. The gang members who did the actual strangling, called *bhutortes*, received a larger share of the booty than the others.

When the Thugs had taken their places among their victims, with the *bhutortes* standing behind them, a signal was given. (A favorite strangler ruse was to get their victims to look at the sky, giving easy access to their necks.) Each bhutorte threw the *ruhmal* around his victim's neck, while assistants known as *shumseeas* (hand-holders) secured his arms and legs. After strangulation, the victim was often stabbed in the eyes to ensure death. The Thugs then took part in a ritual feast of unrefined sugar, or *gur*, after which the bodies were searched thoroughly and the spoils distributed. Finally, the bellies of the dead were slashed and they were buried or thrown into wells.

THE THUG-HUNTER

During the 1820s, some Indians were making fortunes from the burgeoning opium trade. Vast amounts of money, gold and other valuables were being transported around the country by 'treasure-bearers.' When a number of Thug gangs made spectacular hauls, the Company was once again forced to take notice.

In 1829, an officer named William Borthwick, stationed near Indore, in central India, learned that a gang of Thugs was camped nearby, and lured seventy of them into a village, where they were arrested. While most protested their innocence, a few confessed. Borthwick had the bodies of some of their victims disinterred, and the Thugs were charged with murder. Shortly after this, the new governor-general of India, William Bentinck, announced a change in Company policy. Previously, its officers had only been able to deal with crimes committed in their own states. Now they were authorized to pursue Thugs wherever they went, even into the native states if necessary.

One man who read Bentinck's announcement with more than usual interest was William Sleeman, who was stationed in Jubbulpore (now Jabalpur), the administrative capital of the then Saugore and Nerbudda territory in central India. Sleeman, who was born in Cornwall in 1788, had arrived in India in 1808. He had spent ten years as a soldier, rising to the rank of captain, before becoming a political officer. It had been a disappointingly uneventful career so far for Sleeman, who saw the anti-Thug campaign as a way to make a name for himself. He was unusually well equipped for the job in that he had a genuine interest in Indian culture, could speak several native languages, including Hindustani and Persian, and was sympathetic to the plight of ordinary Indians.

Learning that a gang of Thugs north of Saugore had—unusually—bungled an operation and let a group of sepoys escape, Sleeman despatched troops who captured about thirty of them. Again, some confessed. Sleeman interrogated them, and the system he developed for dealing with Thug informants, known as approvers, was soon adopted across India. Transcripts were made of the interviews, during which the approvers were required to describe in detail their involvement in Thuggee. They were assured that if they told all they knew, their lives would be spared. Sleeman found that many knew about the activities of gangs other than their own, and realized that here was the means to crush the Thugs.

Approvers were asked to identify Thugs among prisoners already in custody. Others were sent out on the roads with troop patrols that had the power to arrest anyone that the approvers pointed to as a Thug. Considerable efforts were made to ensure that these accusations were corroborated. The approvers were also required to pinpoint the burial places of victims, which they did time and time again. Eventually, hundreds of bodies were recovered. As more information flowed in, Sleeman compiled extensive lists of Thug crimes and their participants, and detailed genealogies of the major Thug families. His biggest coup was the arrest in late 1830 of Feringeea, one of the most charismatic and successful *jemadars*. Feringeea's family had been involved in Thuggee for generations, and he had an encyclopedic knowledge of the gangs and their crimes. The information he provided led to the arrest of hundreds of Thugs. In 1836, Sleeman was appointed Superintendent for the Suppression of Thuggee, with authority over the entire subcontinent. Just four years later, he was able to announce that the gangs had been routed, and Thuggee eliminated.

The campaign caused a great sensation throughout the British Empire. Philip Meadows Taylor's 1839 novel *Confessions of a Thug* was a huge bestseller, eagerly read by Queen Victoria while still at proof stage. The British were horrified by the brutality of the stranglers and the lack of remorse they showed, but were also surprised to find that the average Thug was, as Sleeman's grandson and chronicler of Thuggee James Sleeman put it, usually 'a good citizen and model husband.' Some developed a grudging respect for the Thugs, who held to their moral code firmly, however twisted it might have been. It was noted that, while they occasionally killed women, they were never disrespectful to them beforehand.

William Sleeman questioned some of the Thugs about their beliefs, and the transcripts of these interviews provide a fascinating insight into their mindset. Some attributed their downfall to breaking Kali's rules (by killing women, for example), while all were adamant that Thuggee was for them a calling they had little power to resist. Speaking of the ceremonial eating of sugar that took place after each killing, Feringeea said:

Let any man once taste of that *gur* and he will be a Thug although he knows all the trades and has all the wealth in the world ... My father made me taste of that fatal *gur* when I was yet a mere boy; and if I were to live a thousand years, I would never be able to follow another trade.

Statements like this convinced Sleeman that Thugs were beyond rehabilitation, and once imprisoned, they were never released, even those who had become approvers.

In all, some 4,500 Thugs were brought to trial during the campaign, and almost all were convicted. About 500 were hanged, and the remainder sentenced to life imprisonment. The unlucky ones, tattooed or branded with the word 'Thug,' were transported in chains to hellish penal colonies in the East Indies. The more fortunate remained in jails in India, where they were popular tourist attractions for decades, always keen to demonstrate to visiting Europeans the old tried and trusted methods of Thuggee.

C⊕NTR⊕VERSIES

The suppression of the Thugs became, for the British, one of the most useful justifications for the colonization of India. As Thugs never attacked Europeans, the Company could point out that its campaign was purely altruistic (although this ignores the fact that its sepoys were regular victims). Over the last few decades, anti-colonialist historians have called into question the accepted picture of Thuggee. They have claimed that the Thug gangs were not as organized as the British claimed, and that most of the men convicted of Thuggee were common bandits. This ignores, however, a vast amount of documentation in British and Indian archives that corroborates the picture of Thuggee built up by Sleeman and his colleagues.

More recently, British historian Mike Dash, while recognizing Thuggee as a genuine, well-organized movement responsible for the deaths of tens of thousands, has called into question the importance of its religious beliefs. He points out that Hindus routinely invoke their gods before an endeavor, just as the Thugs sought the blessing of Kali, and argues that their motivation was pure greed. Nevertheless, the fact remains that murder in India during the time of the Thugs was, apart from the crimes carried out by the Thugs themselves, relatively uncommon, and Thuggee involved a coming together of religion and murder virtually without parallel in history. It is clear from Sleeman's interviews with Thugs that they believed their actions were not only sanctioned but ordered by Kali, and it seems certain that, without that belief, many of them would never have turned to murder.

DANCES
with snakes

Serpent Handlers/
The Church of God
With Signs Following

(Began c. 1910)

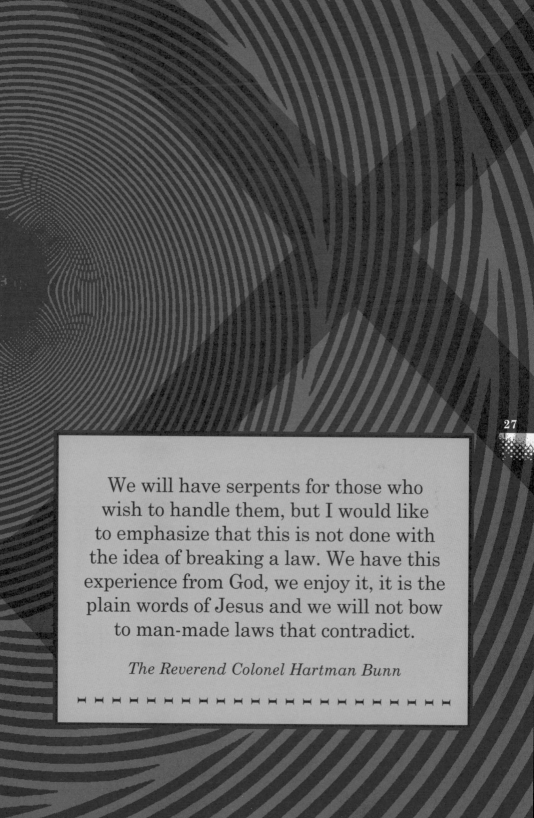

We will have serpents for those who
wish to handle them, but I would like
to emphasize that this is not done with
the idea of breaking a law. We have this
experience from God, we enjoy it, it is the
plain words of Jesus and we will not bow
to man-made laws that contradict.

The Reverend Colonel Hartman Bunn

ONE DAY—THE DATE IS STILL UNCERTAIN, ALTHOUGH IT WAS AROUND 1910—an itinerant preacher named George Went Hensley went out and caught himself a rattlesnake.

Hensley, who was in his late twenties and lived in Grasshopper Valley, Tennessee, had been thinking about a curious passage in chapter 16 of the Gospel of Mark. Just prior to his ascension, Jesus declares:

And these signs shall follow them that believe; In my name shall they cast out devils; they shall speak with new tongues; They shall take up serpents; and if they drink any deadly thing it shall not hurt them; they shall lay hands on the sick, and they shall recover.

Like most members of the Pentecostal/Holiness churches that had sprung up in America, particularly in the southern states, since the mid-nineteenth century, Hensley was inclined to interpret the Bible quite literally. The ecstatic babbling in strange languages known as 'speaking in tongues' had been a part of Pentecostal services since the 1890s when it first occurred spontaneously at a meeting in North Carolina. Why, then, should believers in Christ not also take up serpents?

The following Sunday, he preached a sermon on the passage from Mark, then reached into a box, brought forth the rattler he had caught and brandished it in the air. He challenged the rest of his congregation to handle the snake, too, lest they be 'doomed to eternal hell'. A new and spectacular tradition had been born.

THE TRAVELING SERPENT SH⊕W

Hensley spent the next few years touring Tennessee, holding services in which snakes were handled, and built up a small following. Again taking his cue from Mark's gospel, he also pioneered the practice of drinking poison (usually a mixture of strychnine and water known as a 'salvation cocktail'). Sometimes unbelievers came to gawp at these proceedings, occasionally bringing snakes with them. During one of Hensley's early services, a box of copperheads, cottonmouths and rattlesnakes was dumped onto the floor by a group of men. According to a witness, Hensley picked them up 'like a boy would gather stovewood in his arms to carry to the house.' Meanwhile, a former Baptist named James Miller had, apparently independently of Hensley, begun to handle snakes in 1912, and spread a separate tradition of the practice through Alabama and Georgia.

Hensley's activities came to the attention of A. J. Tomlinson, a former Bible salesman who had founded the fundamentalist Church of God in 1903. He invited Hensley to give a demonstration, was greatly impressed, and ordained him as a pastor. Snake handling quickly spread through the Church of God, but enthusiasm for it waned after 1918, when one handler was bitten and took several weeks to recover (it was also around this time that an Alabama man, Jim Wiley Reece, became the church's first recorded casualty). Hensley, having marital problems, dropped out of snake handling at this point. He became what they referred to as a 'backslider,' made moonshine whiskey and spent time in jail. He bounced back in 1932, arriving in Kentucky with a new wife and a renewed fervor to take up serpents. Previously unknown in Kentucky, the practice quickly spread through the state.

Snake handlers got their first real publicity in 1938, when a farmer who didn't want his wife handling snakes brought a suit against three members of the Church of God in Pine Mountain, Kentucky. They were acquitted, but a reporter and a photographer were despatched by a Saint Louis newspaper to cover one of the Pine Mountain services. They found seventy-five worshippers crammed into the wooden church, singing hymns, pounding out the rhythm with hands, feet and tambourines. Their bodies jerked and shook as they passed snakes to each other. All took part, with even a baby observed touching a snake. Some of the men were also practicing 'fire handling,' which is often seen in snake-handling services, and usually involves participants putting their hands in an open flame from a lamp or torch.

In 1943, snake handling was brought back to Grasshopper Valley, Tennessee, by a preacher and disciple of Hensley's, Raymond Hayes. A church was built, with rough timber walls and an earthen floor, and named the Dolly Pond Church of God With Signs Following. Tom Harden became its pastor and presided over services most Saturday and Sunday nights, at which many snakes were handled and faith in God vigorously affirmed. It was here, in September 1945, that a thirty-two-year-old truck driver named Lewis Ford was bitten and became the next casualty of the cult. Ford's funeral was attended by 2,500 people; snakes were handled over his coffin and his father Walter, a church deacon, rubbed his face with them.

Two weeks later, Tom Harden, George Hensley and other members of the congregation went to Chattanooga and began holding meetings in a tent on the outskirts of the city. When the crowds grew so big that traffic was disrupted, policemen moved in and arrested Harden and Hensley. They were charged with disorderly conduct and fined $50 each, which they refused to pay. They did some time on a road gang, but the charges were eventually dropped.

In February 1947, following a spate of deaths, the state of Tennessee banned snake handling. The handlers refused to bow to the laws of man, and at one point the entire congregation at Dolly Pond was arrested. They laughed and sang as they were carted off to the local courthouse; their snakes were confiscated and killed. Faced with persecution in Tennessee, the movement spread to other states, including Virginia and North Carolina.

In North Carolina, the cult centered on the Zion Tabernacle in Durham and its self-appointed minister, the Reverend Colonel Hartman Bunn. In October 1948, Bunn was charged with violating a city council ordinance against the public handling of snakes. He remained defiant, and announced to reporters that a three-day interstate conference of snake handlers would take place in Durham, beginning Friday 15 October.

Snake handlers from the surrounding states converged on Durham for the convention. On the first evening, police raided a service at the Zion Tabernacle and confiscated four copperheads and a rattlesnake (an enterprising policeman had earlier made a pair of long-handled forceps for this purpose). Bunn jokingly offered his help in catching them, then asked to be arrested, but the police declined. They did not intervene the following night, when a spirited service was held, with Bunn brandishing snakes and draping them over his head. On the Sunday afternoon, the meeting moved to a spot outside the city limits and police jurisdiction.

Bunn said he had a particularly large snake he did not want the police to get, and one of the news photographers present had asked to see snake handling in a more rural setting than the Zion Tabernacle. The snake handlers performed enthusiastically from the back of a truck as newsreel cameras and photographers captured it all. One snake handler apologized to a reporter, saying his usual specialty was poison drinking, but he had not had enough time to obtain any strychnine.

VANQUISHING EVIL AND GAINING IMMORTALITY

Pentecostal services are famously lively affairs. Pentecostals emphasize the importance of a vibrant, personal connection to God, and their services are characterized by ecstatic singing and praying, 'speaking in tongues,' fainting or convulsing (known as 'slaying of the spirit'), prophesying and healing by the 'laying on of hands.' In this context, snake handling—and poison drinking—are simply slightly more dramatic ways of affirming one's faith in the Lord.

Weston La Barre, an anthropologist who studied snake handlers in the 1950s, noted that snakes are ubiquitous in myths and legends across the world. They are often connected to the concept of immortality, there being a common folk belief that snakes can endlessly regenerate themselves by sloughing off their dead skins. In Genesis, God withholds his initial promise of eternal life to Adam and Eve when Eve is tempted by the serpent, and it took the coming of Jesus Christ for the promise to be fulfilled.

Snakes appear in many guises in the Bible. While they are often symbols of evil and death, they can also represent knowledge, wisdom or the power of God.

In the Old Testament Book of Numbers, it is recorded that, following the Exodus from Egypt, the Jews began to question God and Moses. To punish them, God sent fiery serpents that bit and killed many.

And Moses prayed for the people. And the Lord said unto Moses, make thee a fiery serpent, and set it upon a pole: and it shall come to pass, that everyone that is bitten, when he look upon it, shall live. And Moses made a serpent of brass, and put it upon a pole, and it came to pass, that if a serpent had bitten any man, when he beheld the serpent of brass, he lived.

With passages like that, the only surprising thing is that people didn't start taking up serpents earlier. (Although La Barre noted that a passage in Ecclesiastes—'Surely the serpent will bite without enchantment, and a babbler is no better'—could be taken as an admonition against both snake handling and speaking in tongues.)

The members of the original snake-handling congregations were fiercely conservative rural folk, distrusting of city people and always on the lookout for evil. They were farmers or miners for the most part, and many of the older ones were illiterate. They did not smoke tobacco or drink alcohol, tea or coffee, and many found carbonated drinks deeply suspect. The men had short hair and were clean shaven. The women shunned cosmetics, perfume and jewelry, wore ankle-length dresses, and never cut their hair. They ignored religious holidays such as Christmas, believing them unscriptural. Anyone who took medicine for an illness was looked on as having insufficient faith, and some refused to wear spectacles. They lived and died in the hands of God, and when the spirit moved them, they picked up poisonous snakes.

THE TRADITI⊕N LIVES ⊕N

A steady stream of deaths by snakebite kept the snake handlers in the headlines during the early 1950s. The victims included a fifty-year-old woman named Ruthie Craig, who held services in her home in Alabama, and sixty-seven-year-old Reece Ramsey, who was bitten three times on the head by a satinback rattler during an outdoor service in Georgia. Ramsey collapsed to the ground and died as the choir sang 'I'm Getting Ready to Leave this World.'

Then, at a service in Florida on Sunday, 24 July 1955, the cult's founder, George Went Hensley, was loading a rattlesnake back in its box when it sank its fangs into his wrist. His arm grew swollen and blackened but, as snake handlers usually do, he refused medical help. Hensley had once boasted that he had 'been bitten four hundred times 'til I'm speckled all over like a guinea hen,' but this time his number was up. He died vomiting blood the following morning.

The practice of snake handling has waxed and waned since Hensley's death, but it has never died out. It is reckoned that there are around forty small congregations scattered through the southeastern states of America, with about 2000 people regularly handling snakes, while a small number of congregations have sprung up in Canada. Their members have retained the strict morality and customs of the original snake handlers. Many belong to families that have been involved in the practice for generations. While the churches are unaffiliated, many snake handlers know each other and intermarry, and the most prominent preachers travel around, taking part in each other's services.

More than a hundred handlers are now on record as having died from snake bites (with a smaller number killed by drinking poison). The deaths of three people in Tennessee and Georgia in 1971 put snake handlers (or serpent handlers, as they prefer to be called) back in the headlines. Shortly after this, a challenge was mounted against Tennessee's ban, based on the First Amendment's guarantee of religious freedom, but the state's supreme court reaffirmed the ban in 1973. Snake handling remains illegal in most of the southeastern states, although prosecutions are all but unknown.

Given the large number of people who have handled snakes over the years, the relatively small number of deaths from it has puzzled some. It used to be rumored that snake handlers rendered their snakes harmless by defanging them or milking their poison before services, but there is no evidence this ever happened. Nor can snakes be hypnotized, or trained not to bite. However, it should be noted that, although some 8000 people in the United States are bitten by snakes every year, only about a dozen die. The snakes most commonly used in snake handling ceremonies are the timber rattlesnake, which is not as deadly as some of its larger cousins, and the cottonmouth, which is less venomous still.

Being bitten is, of course, a regular hazard of snake handling. Some handlers talk of a state of 'perfect anointing,' in which the handler becomes so full of the Holy Spirit that he or she can't be bitten, but most handlers dismiss this as nonsense. 'The Bible didn't say they wouldn't bite,' explained Spencer Evans, a twenty-three-year-old preacher recovering from a bite that almost killed him in 1996. Some of the older handlers have been bitten so many times that their hands are deformed and missing fingers.

But what of those who died after being bitten? Surely this makes a mockery of the whole practice. The handlers have various explanations. Perhaps the person wasn't in the right spirit, a 'backslider,' or God had decided that it was their time to be taken away. Ultimately, though, what happens after someone picks up a serpent is irrelevant. The command to take up serpents and drink deadly things is clear and unequivocal, the very last words that Christ uttered before leaving Earth. If the Bible's every word is true, then believers must make sure it stays true. And on top of these religious convictions, there is unmistakably some of the stubbornness, pride and rebellious spirit characteristic of the American South.

On Saturday, 3 October 1998, the Reverend John Wayne 'Punkin' Brown was preaching at a revival meeting at Rock House Holiness Church in Alabama when a four-foot yellow timber rattlesnake bit the middle finger of his left hand. Brown, who was thirty-four, was a legendary evangelist who had been handling snakes since the age of seventeen. He was known to wipe the sweat off his forehead with a rattler, and had been bitten twenty-two times before. He kept preaching for a further fifteen minutes before he collapsed and died. His wife, Melinda, had died in similar circumstances in Georgia three years earlier. Brown left behind five children.

Punkin Brown's colleagues were, as usual on these occasions, sanguine about his demise. 'It was the hand of God. It was his time to go,' commented a fellow pastor, the Reverend Carl Porter from Georgia.

'A lot of people don't understand us,' added the Revered Glen Sherbert. 'We are just normal people but we believe God's word.'

APOCALYPSE
in Waco

The Branch Davidians
(Founded 1929)

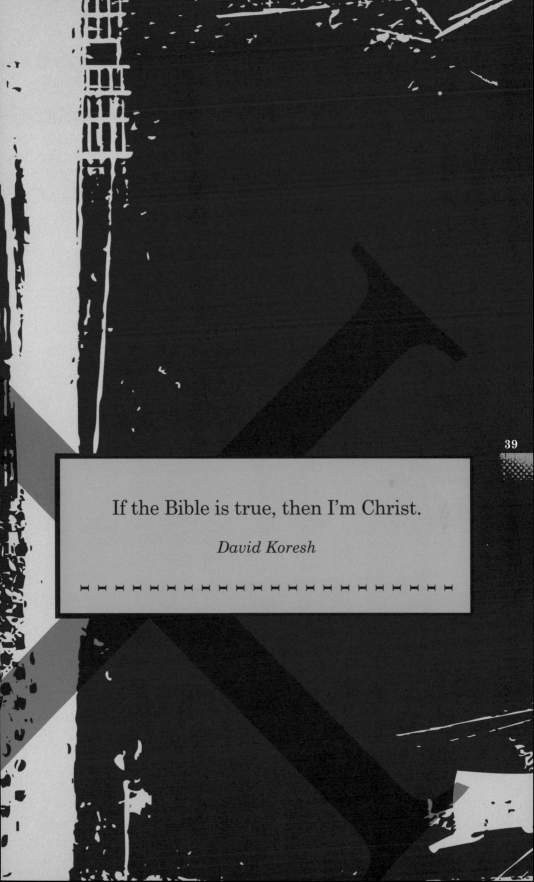

If the Bible is true, then I'm Christ.

David Koresh

ON THE MORNING OF SUNDAY, 28 FEBRUARY 1993, a convoy of vehicles arrived at a sprawling wood and sheet-rock complex 10 miles out of Waco, Texas. As helicopters swooped overhead, the back doors of two cattle trucks fell open and from them poured agents of the Bureau of Alcohol, Tobacco and Firearms, wearing helmets and bullet-proof vests, and armed with shotguns and semi-automatic rifles.

The inhabitants of the complex watched from the windows as they arrived. They had been waiting for them a long time. Their coming had, in fact, been foretold thousands of years ago, in the Bible. The conflict, they believed, would end with the ascent into heaven of their leader, David Koresh, and the creation of God's kingdom on Earth. As they watched the armed men running towards them, it seemed that everything Koresh had told them was true.

'HEAR YE THE R⊕D'

Koresh's group, usually known as the Branch Davidians, began as an offshoot of the Seventh-Day Adventists. Victor Houteff was a Bulgarian immigrant and a teacher in an Adventist school in Los Angeles, but some of his interpretations of the Bible differed markedly from those of the church hierarchy. He believed that in the lead-up to Christ's return, which was imminent, God would send angels to slay all but the most righteous, leaving just 144,000 Adventists to attain the kingdom of Heaven. In 1930, Houteff set out his ideas in a book, *The Shepherd's Rod*, and declared that God had sent him to reform the Adventist church, which had become impure. Its leaders were less than impressed with all this and expelled him.

Houteff continued to preach and drew an increasing number of followers from the Adventists. In 1935, he established a headquarters outside Waco, Texas, which he named the Mount Carmel Center. The group was known as The Shepherd's Rod, but when World War II began and Houteff wanted his followers to be eligible for conscientious objector status, he incorporated it under the name Davidian Seventh-Day Adventists. ('Davidian' refers to King David, whose throne Jesus will occupy upon his return.)

Houteff's wife, Florence, took over the leadership after his death in 1955. She then made a serious miscalculation by issuing a prophecy of her own—that the Second Coming would take place in 1959. The sect embarked on a huge publicity campaign to promote this, with cars driving around bearing large signs proclaiming 'Hear Ye The Rod.' Hundreds of followers quit their jobs, sold all their possessions and made their way to Mount Carmel to await the big event. When it failed to happen, many left the sect and those that remained split into factions. Florence Houteff eventually sold Mount Carmel to Benjamin Roden, the leader of the largest splinter group. Roden, who had received a revelation that the new name of Jesus was 'The Branch,' called his group the Branch Davidian Seventh-Day Adventists. (He came up with a snappy slogan, too—'Get off the dead Rod and move onto a living Branch.') Roden's most notable achievement during his leadership was to establish a small commune of Adventist immigrants in Israel.

Roden died in 1978 and his widow, Lois, took over. Shortly before this, she had created a stir among members with a revelation that the Holy Spirit was female. Not all of the community were happy about her leadership, least of all her son, George, who believed that it was his right to take his father's place as the Living Prophet. As the power struggle between them became increasingly bitter, a new member, Vernon Howell, arrived at Mount Carmel.

THE ROCK 'N' ROLL MESSIAH

Vernon Howell was born in Houston, Texas, in 1959. The illegitimate son of Bonnie Clark, who was fourteen when she gave birth to him, he was raised by his maternal grandparents. A dyslexic, he fared badly at school, where he was nicknamed 'Mr Retardo.' His knowledge of the Bible was phenomenal, however (he had memorized the New Testament by the age of twelve). He also played guitar, and had dreams of becoming a rock star.

Howell joined the Seventh-Day Adventists when he was eighteen, but his rebellious nature (which included wanting to grow his hair long) and idiosyncratic biblical interpretations led to his expulsion, just like Victor Houteff before him. In 1981, he arrived at Mount Carmel. He made no secret of the fact that he was a sinner (compulsive masturbation being just one of his sins), but was soon butting heads with George Roden over the leadership. Howell was able to easily beat the boorish and hot-headed George in scriptural debates, and strengthened his claim for leadership by taking the sixty-seven-year-old Lois Roden as his lover. The pair announced that they intended to have children, and in 1985 traveled to Israel, where Howell believed the Apocalypse would begin. He also increased his status by taking as his first wife fourteen-year-old Rachel Jones, the daughter of one of the sect's elders. She would bear him two children, a boy, Cyrus, and a girl, Star.

George was infuriated by all of this and took to walking around Mount Carmel with an Uzi sub-machinegun on his shoulder. The community split into two factions, with George's faction eventually forcing out Howell and his supporters. They wandered aimlessly around Texas for a while, then settled in a makeshift camp about 100 miles from Mount Carmel. Here, Howell took on a second wife, seventeen-year-old Robyn Bunds, whose parents were long-term sect members.

Lois Roden died in 1986, but her son's hold on the Mount Carmel community remained tenuous, and Howell was still pressing his own claims. George Roden challenged him to a macabre competition to settle the matter once and for all—each would attempt to raise a former Branch Davidian from the dead. The first to do so would be declared Living Prophet.

Howell refused to take part in the contest, but Roden went ahead with it anyway and dug up the coffin of Anna Hughes, who had died twenty-five years previously, aged eighty-five. It was placed on an altar, a flag with the Star of David was draped over it, and Roden spent several days praying and uttering incantations, without any significant success. Vernon Howell, thinking laterally, went to the police in Waco and told them that Roden was abusing a corpse. He was informed that no action could be taken unless they had evidence, so Howell decided to get a photograph of the grisly display.

Early one morning, Howell and seven accomplices arrived at Mount Carmel. They were dressed in camouflage gear and heavily armed. After waiting for the adults who had day-jobs to leave, Howell and his men made their way in. Roden, alerted to their presence, grabbed his Uzi and went to meet them. A twenty-minute shoot-out followed, during which Roden was wounded in the chest and hand but, amazingly, no one else was injured. Sheriff's deputies eventually intervened, and Howell and his men gave themselves up.

At the subsequent trial for attempted murder, Howell denied aiming at Roden, and said that his men had only fired into the air to intimidate him. Anna Hughes, in her coffin, made a guest appearance as an exhibit. The jury failed to come to a unanimous verdict on Howell, and the judge declared a mistrial. Two of the jurors were so impressed with Howell that they went up and hugged him afterwards. Later, the charges against him were dropped, while his accomplices were acquitted.

Meanwhile, George Roden had managed to land himself in prison. The leadership tussle with his mother had ended up before the courts and, unhappy with a decision by the Texas State Supreme Court, Roden filed a number of further matters. In one of them, he suggested that unless the judges came down on his side, God would smite them with herpes and AIDS. He was charged with contempt of court and sentenced to six months in jail. The way was open for Vernon Howell to return to Mount Carmel as its undisputed leader.

RANCH AP⊕CALYPSE

Howell immediately put his stamp on the ramshackle compound, which was littered with rubbish and the bodies of abandoned cars. The place was cleaned up, rickety walls were torn down or strengthened, and new ones built. A watchtower was erected. Tunnels were dug between the buildings, and a bus was buried to make a rudimentary bunker. Conditions remained primitive, however, in what was essentially one enormous rabbit warren of a house. There was no central heating or air conditioning, and only the kitchen had plumbing. Howell liked the fact that Mount Carmel was rambling and unfinished, as it reflected his ideas about spirituality. He shared the Adventist belief that

Christianity was something that constantly changed and evolved as God spoke through the people he had chosen to be his prophets.

Howell also imposed order on the lives of his followers. They were expected to live communally and donate all their income to the group. Their diet consisted of meager portions of cereal, fruit and vegetables. They rose every day before dawn, exercised for ninety minutes, then spent the rest of the day either working or attending Bible classes. These Spartan living conditions did not apply to Howell, who often slept in until the afternoon, ate what he wanted, drank beer and took up smoking at one point. When questioned about this, the Living Prophet, who had a biblical answer for everything, quoted a description of God from Psalm 18: 'There went up a smoke out of his nostrils.'

Howell could have talked about the Bible under wet cement. Sometimes his classes went for sixteen or seventeen hours. His followers, already exhausted by their long day, would have to listen until well after midnight as he spouted scripture and talked of the end of the world. At other times, they were treated to performances by Howell's rock band, Messiah.

Vernon Howell had come to believe that he was the seventh angel put on Earth to usher in God's kingdom. Central to his thinking were passages in the Book of Revelation concerning a scroll with seven seals, the opening of which would initiate the Apocalypse. Revelation identifies a Lamb as the only one who can open the seals. Most Christians assume this is Jesus, but Howell claimed that he was the Lamb, and his sinfulness was an integral part of this role. The first Messiah had been without sin, but the new one, having tasted all temptations, would make a much better judge of good and evil. He had also come to believe that the Apocalypse might begin in Texas rather than Israel, and in anticipation of a violent struggle started to stockpile weapons and food.

In August 1989, Howell announced that he had received a new revelation. God had instructed him to produce an army of children from his own seed, and he had the right to take any female in the sect as his wife, regardless of whether they were already married or under the age of consent. Male followers were, on the other hand, to remain celibate, and sleep in separate quarters from the women. (He consoled them with the thought that each would, upon his resurrection, receive a perfect partner made from one of his own ribs.)

This announcement caused great consternation among his followers, especially the married couples. Some left. Others, after much soul searching, agreed to his proposal. Howell eventually took on nearly twenty wives and fathered seventeen children. One of his wives was aged twelve; another was Jeanine Bunds, the fifty-year-old mother of his second wife Robyn. Disgusted by this turn of events, Robyn walked out.

In 1990, Vernon Howell legally changed his name to David Koresh. David came from King David, while Koresh is the Hebrew form of Cyrus, the Persian king who allowed the Jews to return to Israel from Babylon.

The Branch Davidians began to refer to Mount Carmel, only half jokingly, as Ranch Apocalypse.

THE BUNGLED RAID

As more people defected from the group, stories about life in Mount Carmel began to circulate. One group of defectors in Australia hired a private investigator, and fed a stream of information to the press and various government agencies, including the FBI. Given Koresh's new policy on taking wives, many were concerned about the underage girls living with him, while some alleged that he was guilty of beating young children and denying them food. Welfare officers visited the compound, but could find no evidence of this.

There was also concern about the stockpiling of weapons. Most of them were legal, but the Bureau of Alcohol, Tobacco and Firearms (ATF) learned that Koresh and his men had been converting semi-automatic rifles into machine guns, which they were not licensed to do. (Survivors of the destruction of Mount Carmel maintain the only reason they were doing this was to sell the modified weapons for a profit.) It was the ATF who eventually decided to take action against Koresh.

It would have been very easy to arrest David Koresh outside the Mount Carmel compound. He could often be seen in Waco and other places, attending gun shows or drinking in rock 'n' roll bars with his high-ranking male followers, the so-called Mighty Men. Instead, the ATF decided that the best way to handle the situation of a compound bursting with arms and ammunition and, as they thought, crazed cultists, was to turn up en masse, themselves heavily armed. It seems that there were budget hearings coming up, and the ATF hoped that the raid would gain them much favorable publicity.

The operation was planned with meticulous care. Arriving at the compound, the ATF personnel would split into groups. Some would move to the area where the women and children lived separately from the men, so as to protect them. Others would enter through a second-floor window, make their way to the armory and secure it. They practiced it all among mock-ups of the buildings. Extra agents were brought in to beef up the numbers. It was a wonderful plan that went awry almost immediately.

Koresh had been tipped off about the raid. As an ATF agent approached the open front doors and called out 'Police! Search warrant! Lay down!', Koresh, who was standing inside the doorway, dressed in black, slammed the doors shut.

It was later a matter of dispute who fired the first shot. Whoever it was, a ferocious gun battle broke out, and the ATF found, to their dismay, that most of the fire was directed at them. They were completely outgunned.

After about forty-five minutes, an ATF agent in phone contact with the compound managed to arrange a ceasefire. Four ATF agents and six Davidians were either killed during the raid or died of injuries soon after. Many more were injured, including David Koresh, who had been shot in the side and in one hand.

That night, Koresh gave a phone interview with CNN. His voice shaking with pain, he said that he had tried to urge the ATF to leave, telling them there were women and children in the compound, and his men had only opened fire after the ATF fired first.

After the debacle of the raid, the FBI took over. A team of negotiators was assigned to talk to Koresh and a few others inside the compound and persuade them to surrender. At first it appeared that this would happen soon, and 3 March was set as a tentative date, following the broadcast of a fifty-eight-minute taped sermon by Koresh over the radio. The sermon was broadcast as promised, but at the last minute, Koresh received a one-word message from God—'Wait.'

INFERN⊕

Outside the compound, around the perimeter set by the FBI, journalists, TV crews and hundreds of curious people were gathered. A circus atmosphere prevailed, with vendors selling T-shirts and Koresh burgers, and religious fanatics of various stripes wandering around holding signs.

The negotiations dragged on. Koresh persisted in talking about the Seven Seals and other theological matters with the FBI men, who were baffled by it all. The wound in his side was obviously causing him a lot of pain, and as the days went by it seemed to the agents that he was becoming more hysterical. He sent out a couple of letters, one of which purported to be from God, warning that the Waco area would be destroyed by earthquake and flood if the government didn't back off. The FBI responded by increasing security around the compound, including bringing in tanks. Loudspeakers were set up which subjected the Davidians to a continuous barrage of sound, from recordings of dental drills and dying rabbits, to Nancy Sinatra singing 'These Boots Were Made For Walking.'

Meanwhile, a continuous stream of people had been allowed to leave the compound, including twenty-nine children and some of the older adults. That left more than twenty children inside, most of them fathered by Koresh.

While the FBI cast Koresh as a liar who had broken his word about the 3 March surrender, Koresh maintained that he was waiting for God to tell him what to do. It appears that he was genuinely puzzled by the situation he was in. He was sure that the raid and siege were all part of the Apocalypse, but the details did not fit his previous interpretations of how it would unfold

49

(he had expected it to start in 1995, for example, not 1993). On 14 April, God finally came through. Koresh announced that he was to write a complete exposition of the Seven Seals that would be released to the world. When that was completed, he and his followers would surrender. He immediately set to work. He had finished writing about the first seal, and was working on the second, when the FBI ran out of patience. The new attorney general, Janet Reno, who had only been in the job for two weeks, authorized the use of gas on the compound. Cult experts had advised the FBI that Koresh and his followers were unlikely to commit mass suicide, as Jim Jones' followers had done at Jonestown. Reno later said that her chief concern was the welfare of the children still inside.

On 19 April, fifty-one days after the siege began, armored combat vehicles began smashing holes in the walls of the compound and pumping CS (tear) gas into the rooms. When some of the Davidians shot at the vehicles, the attack was stepped up, and tanks were used to fire canisters of gas into the buildings. Inside, Koresh's followers, wearing gas masks, tried to go about their daily routine. Women did the laundry, others attended Bible class. Then, just after midday, a fire broke out.

As thousands of people watched the live television coverage, the fire, whipped by winds of 30 mph, spread through the flimsy compound with astonishing speed. Nine of the Davidians were able to escape the burning buildings. About eighty others, including Koresh and all of the remaining children, were incinerated.

The horrifying end to the siege led to much recrimination and controversy, which continues to this day. The FBI remains adamant that the Davidians started the fire. The agency notes that three fires seem to have been ignited simultaneously, suggesting arson, and produced transcripts of muffled recordings from inside the compound that had people saying things like 'Spread the fuel around.' The survivors vehemently deny that they had planned to commit suicide. They say that the fires started when lanterns were knocked over during the attack (lanterns had been used for lighting since the government cut off the compound's electricity early in the siege) and these set fire to bales of hay that had been placed against walls to stop bullets. After initial denials, the FBI admitted that some pyrotechnic devices were used in the operation (designed to release CS gas), but maintained that these were deployed four hours before the fires broke out. Autopsies showed that twenty Davidians had been shot (including Koresh), but whether this was by FBI sharpshooters, as some claim, or by the Davidians themselves, is impossible to determine. With so much of the physical evidence destroyed in the conflagration, the full story of what happened to David Koresh and his followers will probably never be known.

51

The Prophet of PROFIT

Mankind United/Christ's Church of the Golden Rule

(Founded 1934)

We invite you to participate in the most ambitious and constructive adventure ever undertaken by the people of any age. We invite you to journey with us into a land of 'universal unselfishness and generosity;'—a land, the inhabitants of which give 'freely' of their individual capabilities and talents for the welfare and happiness of all.

from Mankind United

In 1934, a book called *Mankind United* went on sale in California. No author was listed, but its purpose was boldly stated on the cover—'To end illiteracy, poverty and war, and to bring the assurance of lasting peace and guaranteed security to the people of every nation.'

Over the next few years, about a quarter of a million people read the book, went to meetings where it was discussed, or joined the movement that sprang from it. Some donated their entire lives and savings to it. And when it all eventually fell apart, one man walked away from it, a very wealthy man indeed.

MANKIND AT THE CROSSROADS

The book revealed the existence of The International Institute of Universal Research and Administration, which was founded on Christmas Day, 1875, by sixty high-minded men and women. With no hope of personal gain, these individuals, known as 'the Sponsors,' pledged their combined fortunes of $60,000 to the organization. Its aim was to introduce the Golden Rule as formulated by Christ—'Do unto others as you would have them do unto you'—into all human relationships. Its enemies were the 'Hidden Rulers,' a cabal of fabulously wealthy, morally bankrupt men who controlled 'the political parties, governments and major utilities and industries of every civilized nation on earth,' and had deliberately engineered all the wars, revolutions and economic depressions of the last few centuries.

Because of the threat posed by the Hidden Rulers and their thousands of spies, the Sponsors had been forced to operate in complete secrecy. They had, nevertheless, built an immense organization with divisions in many countries. They had done extensive research into the causes of war and poverty, and produced a 100-point program to eliminate them. They had recruited hundreds of idealistic young men and women, the 'Vigilantes,' who would put the program into place. In their research laboratories, they had produced an incredible array of inventions which could be used to fight the Hidden Rulers and revolutionize the world economy.

The Mankind United program had been finalized by 1919, but there were concerns that human beings weren't ready for it. The Sponsors had therefore come to a decision. One division of the Institute's Registration Bureau, the Pacific Coast Division of North America, had been authorized to make public the bare details of the plan. If enough people showed their support for it, the Institute would embark on a thirty-day educational program, utilizing all modern methods of communication, including television and motion pictures, to inform humanity of the Institute's plan and its amazing technological advances. The program would then be put to a worldwide vote, and if 200 million were in favor of it, the Universal Service Organization would be established. This would be a vast cooperative owned equally by all who worked for it, which would eventually employ everyone on Earth. The Institute's inventions would cause productivity to increase a hundredfold. People would only have to work four hours a day, four days a week, and would be guaranteed a minimum wage. They would have eight weeks of paid holidays a year, and a pension after the age of forty. Everyone would live in a beautiful, air-conditioned house with all modern conveniences including 'fully perfected television equipment,' a swimming pool and a garden. 'Limited-use money' would be introduced which had to be spent within a certain time, thus preventing the accumulation of wealth. With people freed from financial worries, most physical ailments would disappear. An 'International Auxiliary Language' would be introduced, so that all the world's people could communicate with each other. Wars would become a thing of the past.

The consequences of not adopting this plan were correspondingly dire. The book warned that the Hidden Rulers were planning another world war, in which 400 million of the world's best educated and most religious people would be slaughtered. One chapter, entitled '40,000 Principalities—One Thousand Million Slaves,' described what would happen after the war. Each of the Hidden Ruler families, of which there were 40,000, would live in a palace atop a 25-storey building. Each building would house 25,000 slaves, the remnants of humanity. The most attractive women among them would be chosen by the Hidden Rulers for their harems. Most of the remainder would be reduced to automaton status, their every move monitored by the rulers on television screens.

It was a terrifying vision, and to register that you would be one of the 200 million who would vote against it, all you needed to do was purchase a copy of *Mankind United*, price $2.50.

THE MAN WHO COULD WALK THROUGH WALLS

Combining a conspiracy theory of stunning simplicity with an appeal to basic Christian values, Mankind United's program proved irresistible to many people hit hard by the Depression. Sales of the book soared, and Mankind United bureaus sprang up across California. Anyone who sold five or more copies of *Mankind United* was invited to start their own '4-4-

56

8-3-4 Club' (the numbers referring to the program's schedule of working hours and holidays). These clubs met in people's homes, while larger meetings were held in storefronts and halls. Several hundred thousand people bought the book, and the Pacific Division leader's claim that there were 27,000 active members in 1939 is plausible.

A great sense of urgency and excitement pervaded the group. The sooner the Pacific Division filled its membership quota, the sooner the thirty-day program could begin. Members urged the book on their friends and co-workers. They were showered with literature from head office giving regular updates on the movement's international growth.

As inspiring as Mankind United's ideals were, many were also attracted by its science-fiction trappings. The movement's literature gave tantalizing glimpses of the fabulous inventions that the Institute had produced, many of which would be used to fight the nefarious Hidden Rulers. There was, for example, a device that stopped motors, and could be used to halt tanks and bring down planes. The Hidden Rulers also had an arsenal of powerful weapons at their disposal, the most dreaded of which was a device that could vibrate people's eyes out of their sockets.

Most Mankind United members believed they had joined a vast worldwide organization. Their only contact with the Institute's hierarchy came in the form of the Pacific Division's leader. Nobody seemed to know his real name, but he was usually referred to as 'The Speaker' or 'The Voice of the Right Idea.' A charismatic individual who could speak for hours without notes, he claimed to have occult powers. He could walk through walls and float through ceilings, and travel to anywhere in the world instantaneously by 'translevitation.' He also had seven 'doubles' scattered across America who looked and sounded exactly like him. They helped him out with his huge workload, and allowed him to chair several meetings simultaneously.

Mankind United reached its peak in 1939, when there were twenty-five active bureaus in Los Angeles alone, but the outbreak of war disappointed many members—they had been assured that the Sponsors had been working behind the scenes to prevent it. Clearly sensing the troubles that were about to descend upon it, the leadership curtailed many of the movement's activities in 1940. Mass meetings ceased, and the *Mankind United* book was no longer distributed. This severely reduced the amount of money coming in, and all members were asked to give $20, which would pay for tuition in the lead-up to the 'thirty-day program.' Demands on the members for money increased over the next couple of years until they were being urged to donate 50 percent of their income.

Many quietly left the movement, and the exodus increased when America entered the war in 1942. With the country throwing itself behind the war effort, Mankind United's denunciation of the 'War Lords' and their 'Fear and Hate-Generating propaganda' had become dangerously subversive, and its claim that Pearl Harbor had been attacked by American planes with Japanese colors didn't help. The FBI, which had been keeping tabs on the movement since 1939 and infiltrated a number of agents into it, pounced on 18 December 1942. The Pacific Division's leader and fifteen others were arrested and charged with sedition. For the first time, Mankind United's members learned that their leader's name was Arthur Bell.

THE PR⊕PHET UNⅢASKED

According to testimony he gave in court, Arthur Lowber Bell was born in New Hampshire on 19 March 1900. His father was a Presbyterian minister who died when Arthur was young. His mother later became a Christian Scientist, and her son also adopted their beliefs. He moved to San Francisco, where he became a successful businessman.

Bell claimed to have been first contacted by the Sponsors in 1919, when he was inducted into the International Legion of Vigilantes. In 1934, while he was on a train, a voice spoke to him in the darkness and told him he had been chosen to unveil Mankind United to the world. From that point on, he had devoted himself tirelessly to the cause, working up to twenty hours a day and letting his business interests slide. He derived no income from the movement, he said, and had only been able to pay for the publication of the *Mankind United* book through the generosity of his second wife, who was independently wealthy.

Bell was a tall, good-looking fellow with a high forehead, dark hair and long sideburns. He wore expensive double-breasted suits and colorful ties, and was by all accounts very popular with the ladies. He never lived with any of the members of the movement, and formed no close personal relationships with them, which only added to his mystique. In his numerous court appearances over the next few years, he stunned investigators with his matter-of-fact descriptions of life in the service of the Sponsors. Sometimes, he said, he would be whisked away to such places as China, and one day he suddenly found himself on a boat in the middle of the Atlantic. 'Do you expect the Committee here to believe this stuff?' spluttered one Senator charged with looking into the movement's financial affairs. Bell was a godsend for reporters, the very image of a smooth-talking, avaricious cult leader.

In May 1943, Bell and five others were convicted and sentenced to five years in prison. Appeals tied up the courts for years, and in 1947, the convictions were overturned on a technicality.

By the time this happened, Bell's movement had taken a new course. In January 1944, he had incorporated a church—Christ's Church of the Golden Rule—and quietly transferred Mankind United's assets to it.

INVITATIⴲN Tⴲ ANⴲTHER WⴲRLD

The remaining members of Mankind United were invited to become 'Student Ministers' in the new church, and about 850 of them agreed. Their commitment was a heavy one. They were expected to donate all their wealth and possessions to the church, and sever all ties with friends and families.

Bell, designated the 'Church Trustee,' went on a real estate spending spree. He bought dozens of properties in California and other states—hotels, office buildings, restaurants, ranches, warehouses, canneries, farms, laundries and many houses and apartments. Each property became the nucleus for a 'project'—a business enterprise run on Mankind United's principles of equality. Student Ministers were assigned to the projects and worked up to twelve hours a day. They weren't paid wages, just given board and $40 a month to buy food and other essentials. They lived in isolation from society and even from the other projects, and read little but church literature. In San Francisco, some 300 ministers and their families lived in a 200-room building known as the San Francisco Seminary Project.

It is impossible to estimate how much income the church's various projects were bringing in. What is certain is that most of it went straight into the pockets of Arthur Bell. He owned several apartments and houses, including a $75,000 mansion overlooking Sunset Strip, which had a 60-foot long living room equipped with a pipe organ. He was known to frequent swanky nightclubs (although he maintained that it was his doubles who were spotted in them).

For a while, there was great enthusiasm among the project workers. They were putting their ideas into practice, showing the way for the Universal Service Corporation which, they fervently believed, would still become a reality one day. But some of the projects proved less successful than others, and some members became disillusioned with the long hours they were working for little reward. A few wrote to the California attorney general, asking how they might extricate themselves from the church and retrieve their investment in it. The attorney general's office launched an investigation.

Then Bell made a serious tactical error, announcing that nine of the church's biggest projects would be put up for sale. This angered many members and prompted the state authorities to act. They applied for the church and its projects to be put into receivership and wound up. Agents began to take over church properties, sometimes by force. Bell retaliated by filing for voluntary bankruptcy.

Over the next six years, Christ's Church of the Golden Rule was gradually devoured by the state of California. Its most profitable properties were sold off to pay legal bills, and by December 1951, when the bankruptcy proceedings were finally settled, little of its business empire remained.

At this point, Arthur Bell announced in a bulletin that he was resigning his position in the church, having been called by the Sponsors for higher things. He left them with some bad news and some good news. The bad news was that the Sponsors had come to the conclusion that human beings would never be ready for the release of the thirty-day plan, and they were withdrawing their offer. They now believed that Earth was doomed.

The good news was that, since the beginning of Mankind United, machines in underground laboratories had been monitoring the thoughts of all those who showed an interest in it, and it had been decided to transport those who had been found worthy to another world. This was a planet almost identical to Earth, and occupying almost the same position, although in another dimension. There were already a few inhabitants there, beings who could communicate telepathically and used thought to build 'practically everything they wish to construct.' It was a world free of war and poverty, just like the Sponsors had always promised. While the equipment that would effect the transition to this world had not yet been perfected, it was advanced enough to be used in the brief moments before a person's death. 'At the very moment that those who believe in your death are arranging to dispose of the body you have abandoned,' wrote Bell, 'you will be fully aware of your re-embodiment, rejuvenation, and transition into the kind of life and world envisioned by Christ Jesus.'

With that, 'The Voice of the Right Idea' left the movement he had created and faded from history. Under his successor, Mrs Adelaide Nordscott, the church went into further decline. More properties were sold off, and by 1956, fewer than a hundred members remained, most of them elderly.

The church did not disappear entirely, though. In 1962, the remaining members bought Ridgewood Ranch, a 5000-acre property in Mendocino County, California, which is famous for its connection to the racehorse Seabiscuit. In the mid-1960s, their neighbors included Jim Jones' Peoples Temple, which had moved from Indiana to the nearby city of Ukiah. Jones' socialist philosophy had much in common with the ideals of Mankind United, and there was even talk of merging the two groups, but the idea was abandoned in 1968. The church remains on the ranch to this day, running a number of businesses according to the Golden Rule.

Mankind United began as a distillation of the political conspiracy theories that have been swirling around the West for centuries (albeit with a refreshing lack of anti-Semitism). By the end, with Bell's promise of a trip to another planet, it had morphed into something like a UFO cult. Looking back on it, many former members had fond memories of Mankind United meetings, and the spirit of idealism that suffused the movement. Yet the fact remains that Arthur Bell was one of the twentieth century's greatest conmen; never have so many human beings been moved to perform such good works by one man's naked greed.

63

SUICIDE
in the jungle

Peoples Temple
(Founded 1954)

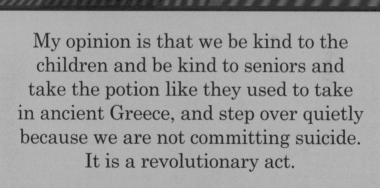

My opinion is that we be kind to the children and be kind to seniors and take the potion like they used to take in ancient Greece, and step over quietly because we are not committing suicide. It is a revolutionary act.

Jim Jones

THE HORRIFYING, SEEMINGLY INCOMPREHENSIBLE SUICIDES AND MURDERS of more than 900 members of Peoples Temple in November 1978 ended what began as a noble social experiment. The smooth-talking, charismatic Reverend Jim Jones gave his followers a vision of a world where all races would live in harmony, property would be shared, and poverty and hunger would disappear. Through the sheer force of his personality he created a large, dedicated and disciplined group who won much praise for their good works. But Jones' desire to dominate his followers became an end in itself. Mounting paranoia led him to leave the United States for the inhospitable jungles of Guyana, where, free of any kind of restraint, his domination became complete.

THE BOY IN THE WHITE SHEET

James Warren Jones was born in Crete, Indiana, on 13 May 1931. His father, also named James, was a disabled war veteran. His mother, Lynetta, sixteen years younger than her husband, was a smart, feisty woman and the breadwinner in the family.

In 1934, they moved to the small town of Lynn. The young Jim Jones was a precocious, bookish loner who discovered early on the power of the spoken word. He used to entertain the local men by swearing, and in return they gave him nickels to buy soda. He was fascinated by religion, and visited all the churches in the area. His favorite was the Gospel Tabernacle, a Pentecostal church on the outskirts of town where the services were wild and the worshippers spoke in tongues. By the time he was ten, Jim was preaching to his school friends in front of a makeshift altar. For a while, he went around with a white sheet over his street clothes, looking like some sort of Eastern holy man. The first signs of Jones'

dominating personality also emerged in these years—
he liked to order other kids around. His best friend, Don
Foreman, later recalled that Jim had twice pointed a
gun at him and fired, narrowly missing him.

Jones' parents separated, and he and his mother
moved to the industrial city of Richmond. He was
working as a hospital orderly when he met a pretty young
nurse named Marceline, and they were married in 1949.
Marceline soon had misgivings about the marriage.
She discovered how possessive and bad tempered
he could be, and was worried when he started telling
people he had lost his faith and thought communism
wasn't such a bad thing. But then he did an apparent
about-face and announced he was going to become a
Methodist minister.

Jones made a name for himself on the Indiana
preaching circuit. Although he had joined the Methodists,
he still leaned towards the flashier Pentecostals, and
was invited to preach at the Lauren Street Tabernacle
in Indianapolis. He practiced 'discerning' (giving people
information about themselves), speaking in tongues
and faith healing. His specialty was the removal
of cancerous growths. He cheerfully faked it all.
(The 'cancers' were animal tissue that Jones appeared to
extract using sleight of hand.)

Lynetta Jones instilled in her son a concern for social
justice, and he was particularly passionate about racial
equality. He dreamed of a church where black and
white could mix easily. Neither the Methodists nor the
Pentecostals were keen on desegregation, however, and
Jones realized he would have to create such a church
himself. He raised funds, and had some success importing
monkeys from South America and selling them door to
door. In 1954, having lured away key members of the

Lauren Street congregation, Jones founded a group called Wings of Deliverance. A year later, he changed the name to Peoples Temple.

THE M⊕VE WEST

Jones' attraction to communism resulted in a philosophy he called 'religious communalism'. He expected his followers to devote their lives and incomes to Peoples Temple. He practiced what he preached, turning his family home into a combination of commune and nursing home for the church's elderly. As well as having a biological son, Stephan Gandhi Jones, he and Marceline created a 'rainbow family' by adopting a Korean boy and girl, and an African-American boy they named Jim Jr. The church received much favorable press coverage in Indiana for its charitable activities, including a free restaurant that served almost 3,000 meals a month in 1960. In the same year, the city appointed Jones as the director of its Human Rights Commission.

Jones had begun to question the Bible and its inconsistencies during his earlier spiritual crisis. Now he began to air such criticisms while preaching. The more conservative Temple members were upset, but others went along with it. Jones was also growing paranoid. He said that Indiana was irredeemably racist, and claimed that his views on desegregation had led to attempts on his life. There was also the matter of an impending nuclear holocaust, which he predicted would happen on 15 July 1967.

In 1965, Jones announced that he was moving his church west, to California, where he claimed they would be safe from nuclear fallout. Many baulked at this, but dozens decided to go, even though it meant leaving their families behind. In July, the group moved to their new home, Ukiah, in California's wine country, where they built a church (with a swimming pool inside it for baptisms), resumed their charitable activities and recruited aggressively. A small number of trusted 'staff members' had the job of secretly digging up information about prospective recruits by infiltrating their homes and going through their garbage. Jones could later bring up this information during church services, thus proving his divine powers.

The Temple expanded to Los Angeles and San Francisco, where it set up shop in the Fillmore ghetto. While still targeting poor African-Americans, it also attracted a number of young, enthusiastic, college-educated whites. Jones and his followers criss-crossed the country in a fleet of buses, collecting donations and drumming up recruits. By 1973, membership had grown to more than 2,500. Jones was a master of networking, and won endorsements from politicians and other officials.

Jones had by now all but abandoned orthodox Christianity. His services still had the format of an old-style revival meeting, with songs, call-and-response-style sermons and the inevitable healing of cancers, but he made no secret now of his contempt for the Bible. He would throw a copy of it on the ground, stomp on it and declare, 'I am God!' Children born into the Temple were baptized 'in the name of Socialism.' His views on sexuality were just as idiosyncratic, and constantly changing. At first he had demanded that his followers remain celibate (and expected the women to have abortions if they became pregnant), but by the late 1960s he was—almost in the same breath—denouncing sexual jealousy between couples and advocating free love. He had sex with many of the Temple's women and impregnated some of them, although only one was allowed to have the baby. Church meetings became a forum for the ribald discussion of individual members' sexuality, with women expected to praise the sexual prowess of Pastor Jones. Meanwhile, Jones often accused his male followers of having homosexual tendencies and, to prove it, sodomized some of them. This did not prevent him from standing up in the pulpit and declaring that he was the church's only true heterosexual.

GUNS AND BARBED WIRE

The occasional racial taunt aside, Peoples Temple had generally been accepted in California. Jones nevertheless continued to warn his followers of the threats they faced. As in Indiana, he seems to have fabricated a number of 'attacks.' (On one occasion he was apparently shot in the chest by a sniper, but managed to save himself by 'dematerializing' the bullet.) Ukiah residents were disturbed to see the church surrounded by a chain-link fenced topped with barbed wire. A small army of gun-toting security guards prowled around it, frisked outsiders before they were allowed to enter, and accompanied Jones wherever he went.

It's true that a few people *were* taking an interest in Peoples Temple. In 1972, the *San Francisco Examiner* began to run a series of critical articles by the paper's religion editor. Jones and his lawyers managed to have the series canceled, but he knew there would be others. He began to think about setting up a refuge outside the United States, and eventually settled on the small, English-speaking South American country of Guyana. The Peoples Temple leased 3000 acres of jungle from the Guyanese government, and a small band of Temple members was sent down to begin clearing the land and building houses.

Jones also laid the groundwork for a mass suicide. One night, during a meeting of the church's governing body, the Planning Committee, he made an exception to one of the rules. Alcohol was usually strictly forbidden, but some excellent wine had been made from grapes grown on a Temple property, and he invited them all to try it. After they had done so, he announced that it contained a poison that would kill them in forty-five minutes. Some committee members collapsed as if dying. One tried to escape (although she may have been acting) and was brought down by a shot from one of Jones' henchmen that later turned out to be a blank. The others stayed where they were. They didn't argue, or ask for an antidote. Jones admitted that there was no poison. He considered the experiment a great success.

While the construction of Jonestown continued, Peoples Temple went from strength to strength. Jones' followers helped the liberal George Moscone become the mayor of San Francisco in 1976, and Jones was awarded with a place on the city's Housing Commission. Peoples Temple supported President Jimmy Carter's election campaign, during which Jones was photographed having coffee with Carter's wife, Rosalynn (a picture that would later cause her much embarrassment). Left wing and progressive groups hailed Jones and his followers as heroes.

There were growing tensions within the church, however. The practice Jones called 'catharsis,' during which individuals were severely criticized by the group, had been a feature of church meetings for years. Now these sessions became increasingly violent, with Jones deciding on punishments—a certain number of blows with a wooden board, for example. Then he had the idea of staging boxing matches, with those who had transgressed (including children) forced to fight bigger, stronger opponents. Some of these bouts resulted in serious injuries. Such developments helped to persuade an increasing number of church members to defect, including long-standing members who knew many of Jones' secrets.

In early 1977, knowing that another investigative article was about to be published in a national magazine, worried by defections and convinced that Internal Revenue and the FBI were on his trail (they weren't), Jones panicked. He announced that the church was moving to the settlement in Guyana, which had been named Jonestown. By September, about 1000 church members, 70 percent of them African-Americans, had gone.

THE PR⊕MISED LAND

Jones had told his followers that Jonestown was the 'Promised Land,' a paradise where the trees were laden with fruit that tasted like ice cream. It was, he said, the perfect place to set up a socialist community. In fact, the soil of Jonestown was infertile, the air thick with flies and other insects, the undergrowth crawling with snakes. It rained almost every day, so that the roads were always muddy, and everything grew damp and mildewed. The township's early settlers had worked heroically, but it was nowhere near ready for such a huge influx of people. Cottages designed for seven or eight people were housing twice that number. Able-bodied church members found they were expected to spend almost every waking moment working. Anyone who refused was beaten by guards or given other punishments, such as being shut up in the 'sensory isolation box,' a wooden shipping crate placed in a ditch, for days on end. Misbehaving children were lowered into a well, at the bottom of which an adult hid, pretending to be a demon.

If Jones thought he was escaping his problems by moving to Guyana, he was mistaken. His greatest danger came in the form of a group of defectors who called themselves the 'Concerned Relatives.' Among these was Tim Stoen, who had been the church's chief attorney and Jones' right-hand man until his defection in 1977. Stoen's wife, Grace, had given birth to a boy, John, in 1972. Shortly after the birth, Stoen had signed a document stating that Jones was the father of the child. Whatever the truth of this, Tim and Grace Stoen mounted a legal battle to have the boy returned from Guyana, which Jones furiously opposed.

One day in October 1977, Jones had one of his men fire shots at the township, and told his followers they were being attacked by armed mercenaries who had come to kidnap John Stoen. A six-day siege followed, during which Jones whipped up hysteria and talked of mass suicide for the cause of socialism.

The siege was the prototype for what became known as 'White Nights.' These would generally begin with Jones bellowing 'Alert! Alert! Alert!' into the community's loudspeaker, the signal for everyone to crowd into an open-air building called the pavilion. Here they were subjected to hours of harangues by Jones while guards armed with guns and crossbows patrolled outside. During one White Night, Jones announced that they were all going to take poison and die. People were lining up to drink what they thought was poisoned fruit punch until Jones' son, Stephan, persuaded him to stop the charade. Stephen and his mother Marceline were now the only ones who could put any sort of check on his behavior.

Despite the overcrowding, Jonestown was initially well organized. Conditions soon deteriorated, however, along with the mental and physical state of its leader.

Jones had been using a variety of prescription drugs since the early days at Ukiah, but his consumption now greatly increased, and he was drinking too. He suffered from a variety of real and imagined ailments, had violent mood swings, and was often irrational. He spent much of his time shut away in the house he shared with two of his mistresses. It had a phone connected to the loudspeaker, and Jones would spend hours talking into it, often slurring his words, reading out the daily news and giving his interpretations. As the once seemingly almighty Jones degenerated into an overweight, shambling mess, the day-to-day running of the community was taken over by a small group of high-ranking white women.

Reports of the horrors of life within Jonestown trickled out. The Concerned Relatives lobbied the U.S. government to take action, but Peoples Temple still had powerful friends, and many within the State Department were reluctant to believe the worst. Then a California Congressman, Leo Ryan, became interested. A pugnacious Irish Catholic and inveterate fighter for just causes, Ryan took what the Concerned Relatives told him seriously. In October 1978, he announced his intention of flying to Guyana on a fact-finding mission.

Jones initially refused to allow Ryan in, but his lawyers persuaded him to change his mind. On the evening of 17 November, Leo Ryan, accompanied by his assistants, nine representatives of the media (including an NBC television crew) and four Concerned Relatives arrived at the entrance to Jonestown.

THE LAST WHITE NIGHT

The following morning, the mood changed dramatically. While none of the four Concerned Relatives had persuaded any of their family members to defect, a few other Temple members told reporters they were ready to go. Jones tried to persuade them to change their minds, without success. He had told Ryan the day before that anyone who wanted to leave was free to do so, but the Temple members around him were looking grim. They knew that even one defection would devastate Jones.

Sixteen defectors came forward. They joined the reporters on the truck that was to take them to the airstrip in Port Kaituma, 6 miles away, where two planes awaited them. Ryan, who had decided to stay an extra day to process more defectors, was in the pavilion when, without warning, a Temple member named Don Sly put a knife to his throat and threatened to kill him. Sly was wrestled away by others, cutting his hand in the process, his blood staining Ryan's shirt. Ryan decided it was time to go, and joined the others on the truck.

At the airport, they began loading the defectors' luggage into the planes. Two Temple vehicles approached, a dump truck and a tractor pulling a trailer holding about a dozen men. They started shooting. Leo Ryan, three journalists and one of the defectors were killed, and another five were severely injured.

Back in Jonestown, most of the community was gathered in the pavilion. Jones sat on his chair on the stage, beneath a sign reading 'THOSE WHO DO NOT REMEMBER THE PAST ARE CONDEMNED TO REPEAT IT.'

'How much I have loved you,' he told them, his words captured for posterity on a tape recorder. 'How much I have tried to give you a good life.' Although he did not know the details of the shootings, he said there had been a catastrophe, and their community was about to be invaded, their children killed. It was time to go.

Only one Temple member, a woman named Christine Miller, tried to reason with him. She asked if they could not escape to Russia (moving the group to Russia or another communist country had been one of Jones' fantasies). She said that the children did not deserve to die. She was shouted down by the others.

A vat containing grape-flavored Flavor Aid (not Kool Aid, as is widely believed) mixed with potassium cyanide was set on a table by the pavilion. The Temple's medical team filled syringes and poured the poison into paper cups.

The children went first. Some resisted and had the poison squirted into their mouths. As they collapsed, convulsing, their parents became hysterical. Jones moved among his people, hugging them and saying goodbye. Some stood to give one last testimonial to their minister. 'I'd like to thank Dad,' said one, 'because he's the only one who stood up for me.' Those who refused to take the poison, such as Christine Miller, were forcibly injected. Many old people were injected without realizing what was happening. Jones urged everyone to die with dignity, but to hurry. 'Quickly! Quickly! Quickly!'

Armed guards patrolled the pavilion to prevent people escaping. One of them, Billy Oliver, was ordered to be the last. He was to make sure that everyone else was dead, then kill himself.

Jones didn't take poison. He was found in the pavilion, the top of his head blown off by a bullet. No-one knows who fired it.

There is no doubt that many Peoples Temple members, including all of the children, were murdered. Many others went to their deaths willingly, though, and their reasons were complex. Some genuinely believed that Jones was God, with the power to heal the sick and raise the dead. Others were no more religious than Jones himself was at the end, and believed in the movement's social ideals. Some eighty Peoples Temple members survived the slaughter (most of them because they were in the United States or the Guyanese capital of Georgetown) and many retain fond memories of Jonestown, despite the hardships and violence.

The relationship that Jones had forged with his people was a symbiotic one. They could see that their leader, like their movement, was sick, probably dying. They were willing to die with him just to stop his suffering. And Jones was unable to conceive that any of them could survive him.

Jones' son, Stephan, who was in Georgetown with the Temple's basketball team on the day of the slaughter, put it more simply. 'He was an overgrown kid, and people were his candy store—and most especially the people in Jonestown.'

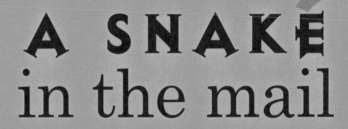

A SNAKE
in the mail

Synanon
(Founded 1958)

Our religious posture is: Don't mess with us—you can get killed dead, literally dead.

Chuck Dederich

On 10 October 1978, an attorney, Paul Morantz, arrived at his home in Pacific Palisades, Los Angeles. Morantz had recently been acting for a number of former members of a drug rehabilitation program turned quasi-religion called Synanon. Knowing that Synanon members had been making threats against him, Morantz had asked the California attorney general's office for protection.

Letting himself in the front door, Morantz noticed something in his mailbox and put his left hand inside to retrieve it. He felt a sharp sting and ran into the front yard, screaming. Someone had placed a $4^1/_2$-foot rattlesnake with its rattles removed in the mailbox. Morantz was rushed to hospital, where he was pumped with anti-venom serum. He survived, but his arm suffered permanent damage.

A suspicious car had been seen in the area that day, and its registration number noted. Police soon traced it to a property owned by Synanon.

PLAYING THE GAME

Synanon was the brainchild of Charles 'Chuck' Dederich, who is reputed to have coined the phrase 'Today is the first day of the rest of your life.' Born on 22 March 1913, in Toledo, Ohio, Dederich held down a variety of jobs, from sales executive with an oil company to manual laborer. A big, blustering man, he became an alcoholic after a mastoidectomy which left his right eye half closed and the right side of his face constantly twitching. In 1956, after his second wife left him, he began attending Alcoholics Anonymous meetings in California. He became an enthusiastic member, speaking at meetings across the state, but fell out with the leadership when he argued that AA should accept drug addicts. After leaving it in 1958, Dederich continued to see others he had met there.

They held meetings in a rented shopfront, at first calling themselves TLC (for Tender Loving Care). This was changed to Synanon, supposedly after Dederich heard an addict stumbling over the words 'symposium' and 'seminar.' It was incorporated as a non-profit foundation in September 1958.

Dederich believed that drug addiction was the result of behavioral patterns that could be changed. The two keys to achieving this were communal living and a technique developed during the group's early days called 'the Game.' This was an intense, no-holds-barred group encounter session, usually lasting two or three hours, which Synanon members participated in at least three times a week, in groups of ten to fifteen. Participants were expected to tell their stories honestly, then face withering criticism from the others. No one was exempt from being in the 'hot seat', even Dederich. The Game could be an emotionally grueling process, but physical violence was forbidden. Synanites made a firm distinction between acceptable behavior within the Game and outside it. While playing it, they were to encouraged to vent their frustrations, hatreds and negative feelings. Out in the real world, or on 'the floor,' as they called it, they were to behave civilly and responsibly. They were to be cheerful, no matter how hard they were working—and Dederich worked them hard.

In 1959, Synanon moved to a former armory on Santa Monica beach. There were now about forty people, mostly long-term heroin addicts, living in the group. Newcomers spent their first two or three days going 'cold turkey,' then were assigned to menial tasks. They lived in dorms and were banned from seeing family or friends for ninety days. As they proved themselves, in the Game and outside it, they were given greater responsibilities.

In the early days, much of their time was spent 'hustling'—soliciting donations of money, food and clothing from sympathetic individuals and organizations. Later, as Synanon became lauded for its work in curing addicts, far more was donated than the group could use. The surplus was distributed to the community, a practice known as 'anti-hustling.'

With its membership largely made up of drug addicts and ex-convicts, Synanon was not always popular with its neighbors, but it also found many supporters. A Democrat senator from Connecticut, Thomas Dodd, visited the center in 1962 and declared, 'There is indeed a miracle on the beach in Santa Monica.' In 1965, Synanon bought the huge, luxurious Casa Del Mar hotel, which became its headquarters. The following year, it opened a center in San Francisco, and centers in other cities soon followed. A number of celebrities joined Synanon, including the jazz saxophonist Art Pepper. There was even a Hollywood movie, *Synanon*, released by Columbia Pictures in 1965. Dederich was played by Edmond O'Brien and Synanites appeared as extras.

Synanon's techniques were similar to a number of therapies developed during the 1960s, and eventually grouped under the term 'the Human Potential Movement.' The movement drew on a variety of sources, including eastern religions, the transcendentalist philosophy of Ralph Waldo Emerson, and Abraham Maslow's humanistic psychology. It stressed the importance of what Maslow called self-actualization, by which he meant people maximizing their potential through reason, creativity, self-awareness and trust in others. He talked of 'peak experiences,' when a person has a blissful feeling of wholeness and oneness with the universe. Dederich believed that drug addicts were people who naturally sought such peak experiences. They were just going about it the wrong way.

Such was the media interest in Synanon that non-addicts began to join during the mid-1960s. 'Game clubs' were opened where 'squares' (as Synanites called non-addicts) could participate in the Game and get a taste of the Synanon lifestyle. While they were not full-timers, club members were expected to forgo alcohol and drugs, and donate as much money as they could. Dederich and his followers came to believe that everyone could benefit from Synanon principles. 'If we can re-direct the lives of dopefiends,' he said, 'we can do anything.'

Dederich had been talking for a while about moving Synanon to the country, where he thought it would be easier to introduce people to new concepts and living arrangements. Several thousand acres were purchased in Tomales Bay, Marin County, and this became Synanon's headquarters in 1967. Dederich moved there with his wife, Betty, an African-American woman who had joined Synanon to cure her heroin addiction. Their wedding in 1963 had been a potent symbol of Dederich's belief in racial equality.

By 1969, almost 1,500 people were living in Synanon centers across America, while as many as 6,000 'squares' regularly played the Game. Synanon was now organized like a corporation, with a board of directors, department heads, general managers and so on (although no one doubted that Dederich, or 'the old man' as he was known, was ultimately in charge). It was a family business, too, with Dederich's children, Charles, Jr. and Jady, appointed as vice presidents, and his brother William a director. A number of businesses were started, including Synanon Sales (later called AdGap), which marketed advertising material such as embossed pencils and coffee mugs.

A VISI⊕N ⊕F UT⊕PIA

In 1968, Dederich announced that addicts would no longer 'graduate' from Synanon. Before this, sixty-five had been declared cured and sent out into the world. They were lauded as heroes and ambassadors for Synanon's rehabilitation programs. Dederich was disappointed that some had gone back to their old ways, but his decision was also symptomatic of a new utopianism flowing through the movement. Dederich had decided that most people were dysfunctional, and Synanon offered the only hope for a better world. There was talk of building a model Synanon City in Marin County. The end of graduation upset many addicts, however. They knew that some addicts *had* started successful new lives outside.

Tensions grew between the addicts and the squares, who were now being encouraged to join the community as full-time members. They were often appointed to the plum jobs, which made some addicts jealous. Many were further incensed when Dederich, having been told by his doctor to give up smoking, declared that all Synanites had to give up. Tobacco had been the only drug tolerated in the community, and the ban prompted many to leave. Other continued to smoke in secret. When they were caught, they had their heads shaved as punishment.

Much of Synanon's program now revolved around the idea of 'integration.' This meant integrating squares and addicts, and people of different races, but also freeing individuals of preconceptions about their roles in society. Members were constantly moved around the various centers and given different jobs. Someone who had trained as an architect might find himself doing manual labor for a few months, then going on to a job in sales. Synanon's leaders were also experimenting with new forms of group encounter. 'The Stew' was an extended version of the Game, played by shifting teams over twenty-four hours. 'The Trip' was an even more intense process lasting three days, involving psychodramas and sleep deprivation. It was played by up to one hundred Synanites, a mix of addicts and squares, and was designed to induce a drug-free high.

Another new development was the taping and broadcast of Game sessions. FM radio networks were set up in Synanon centers so that everyone could hear the sessions as they were played out. In an Orwellian touch, Dederich had his office set up so that he could talk to anyone within the Marin County center via its FM network.

By 1974, Synanon had ceased to bear any resemblance to a conventional drug rehabilitation program, and was at risk of losing its tax-exempt status. It applied to the government for recognition as a church. In some ways, this fitted the direction it had been moving. The Game and other group encounter sessions had taken on mystical trappings, with participants wearing ceremonial robes, burning candles and incense, and even playing with ouija boards. There were Synanon prayers and hymns. Much of this was consistent with the transcendental nature of Dederich's teachings. Yet Synanon's critics— as well as many within the group—saw its transformation into a religion as little more than a ploy to help its commercial interests.

Synanon's attempt to be recognized as a church— which ultimately failed—had an unintended consequence. It continued to benefit from the goodwill it had built up during the 1960s, and still received substantial donations. But once it declared itself a church, many started labeling it a cult. Over the next few years, Synanon seemed to do everything possible to live up to this new label.

VASECT⊕ΠIES AND VI⊕LENCE

In 1975, some of the men in Synanon started to shave their heads. This became a sort of craze within the movement, and in a spirit of female equality, Betty Dederich encouraged the women to follow suit. Soon, most members had shaved heads. While this was not something that the leadership had imposed, the sight of shaven-headed Synanites, dressed in their habitual garb of overalls, became a potent symbol for the group's critics.

The following year, Dederich announced that Synanites would no longer have children. This was supposedly to help fight overpopulation, but in a talk entitled 'Children Unmasked,' Dederich noted that 'there's no profit to this community raising our own children.' Pregnant women were told to have abortions, while men who had been members for five years or more were ordered to have vasectomies. About 250 men complied, with some of the operations performed during 'clipping parties.' Dederich was not among them.

In April 1977, Betty Dederich died of lung cancer. She was a much-loved figure within Synanon, and acted as a brake on some of her husband's wilder notions. Chuck Dederich fell into a deep depression, but quickly snapped out of it and two months later married a much younger woman. Shortly after this, he announced that all couples in Synanon, married or not, had to change partners. (He told a reporter, 'Wouldn't it be fun to perform some emotional surgery on people who were getting along pretty well?') Of course, many left, but others tried to make it work, and there were a few mass weddings.

The most disturbing development during these years was the advent of violence within the group. Synanon had always espoused non-violence—after all, one of the purposes of the Game was to allow people to work out their aggressive feelings, making violence unnecessary in real life. The first exceptions to this came when corporal punishment was allowed in Synanon schools, and the situation grew worse during the mid-1970s, when Synanon agreed to take in large numbers of juvenile delinquents who had been referred to them by agencies. These children, some as young as ten, were placed in 'punk squads' and subjected to rigid discipline and physical punishments.

Synanon was now coming under sustained attack from the media, and facing a number of lawsuits brought by former members. It became litigious, especially after it won $600,000 in an out-of-court settlement with the *San Francisco Examiner* (this entered the *Guinness Book of Records* as the then largest libel settlement in history). Synanon, with a forty-strong legal team, went on to sue *Time* for $76 million after the magazine described it as a 'kooky cult' in 1977, although they did not succeed.

Dederich had decided it was time to stop 'turning the other cheek,' and Synanon began to buy weapons and ammunition in large quantities. Two grandly named (if in practice rather inept) security forces were formed, the National Guard and the Imperial Marines. In an atmosphere of mounting paranoia, several ex-members, known as 'splittees,' were beaten up, and one was almost killed. The violence culminated with the planting of the rattlesnake in Paul Morantz's mailbox. Morantz had represented several ex-members seeking custody of children still in the group, and had recently won a judgment of $300,000 against it after a woman claimed that she had been kidnapped and held against her will.

Police raided a Synanon property and seized several tapes. On one of them, entitled 'The New Religious Posture,' Dederich said, 'I am quite willing to break some lawyer's legs and next break his wife's legs and threaten to cut their child's arm off. That is the end of the lawyer. That is a very satisfactory, humane way of transmitting information ... I really do want an ear in a glass of alcohol on my desk. Yes indeed.' While Dederich's defenders tried to explain this as the sort of hyperbole usually spouted in the Game, he was arrested, along with two Synanon members, Lance Kenton and Joe Musico. They were eventually jailed for a year each for planting the snake. (Kenton, the son of bandleader Stan Kenton, had been in Synanon since the age of ten.)

BACK T⊕ THE B⊕TTLE

The rattlesnake incident resulted in an enormous amount of negative publicity for Synanon. The leadership realized they had gone too far and called a halt to the violence. The group was changing in other ways, as well. Dederich had re-discovered hedonism.

Until now, the emphasis in Synanon had been on living communally and simply. Few members had many possessions. However, Dederich and other executives had been paying themselves hefty salaries for some time. With membership dwindling and Synanon's businesses— which now employed many non-members—booming, Dederich decided the time was right to experiment with affluence. A new community was established in Badger, California, where Synanites would receive salaries and live in comfortable apartments with all mod cons.

Many older members saw this as the death of Synanon as a socially progressive movement. Perhaps mindful of this, Dederich embarked on a bold new venture— the Synanon Distribution Network. The idea was to take surplus and damaged stock from corporations and distribute it to non-profit organizations, giving the corporations a tax break and Synanon a small profit. Dederich had such high hopes for this that he moved its headquarters to Washington DC, where he hoped to start a partnership with the federal government. Though it should hardly have come as a surprise to them, the Synanites were greeted with suspicion and surveillance. The plan was abandoned, and Dederich and some of the other leaders went on an extended holiday to Europe, where they started drinking again. News of this sent shockwaves through the movement. 'It's the end of Synanon,' said one member. 'The old man never does anything in moderation.'

Dederich was fined $10,000 for his involvement in the rattlesnake attack. He was ordered to take no further part in the administration of Synanon, although he continued to wield considerable influence. He drank heavily throughout the 1980s (as did many Synanites) and suffered a number of strokes. With his behavior becoming increasingly erratic, he was finally stripped of all authority by the board in 1987. Synanon's membership continued to dwindle, falling to 370 in 1988. The final blow came the following year, when it failed to regain tax-exempt status, and was hit with a bill for $17 million in back taxes. It was forced to sell off most of its businesses and properties. In 1991, Synanon was officially dissolved.

Former members continue to work for companies founded by Synanon, while others have gone into social work. They are divided about the legacy of Dederich, who died aged 83 in 1997. They continue to believe in Synanon's early ideals, but many are angry at Dederich's betrayal. It seems he is as confounding a character to them as to anyone else. One described him as 'the most evil man I have ever met but also the man with the greatest heart for the needy I have ever met.'

Enlightenment
IN ⊕RANGE

Rajneeshism
(Founded 1964)

I've never asked anybody whether I'm right or wrong. Wrong or right if I want to do it, I will do it and I will make it right.

Bhagwan Shree Rajneesh

Bhagwan Shree Rajneesh will always be remembered as the holy man who owned ninety-three Rolls-Royces. A smiling guru who encouraged sex and dancing, he advocated a unique combination of Eastern spiritualism and Western materialism that proved irresistible to many during the 1970s. He traveled to America to found a new community based on his principles, where all would work together and in the process find themselves.

Somehow it ended up more like a concentration camp. Amid mounting paranoia, death threats and the worst mass poisoning in U.S. history, a dream to which thousands had given their lives collapsed.

'I HAVE COME TO WAKE YOU UP'

Rajneesh was born Chandra Mohan Jain on 11 December 1931, in the village of Kuchwada, in Madhya Pradesh, central India. His father, a cloth merchant, was an adherent of Jainism, which teaches non-violence, vegetarianism and chastity, and is traditionally tolerant of other religions. He was brought up by his maternal grandparents, who doted on him, and his grandfather gave him the name 'Raja' (Hindi for 'king'), from which Rajneesh was derived. His grandfather's death, when Rajneesh was seven, was a terrible blow to him. Later, he resolved to steel himself against death, vowing that it would never again affect him.

The young Rajneesh was a sickly, bookish boy who read religious scriptures, guides to yoga and hypnotism, and the works of the great Russian novelists. When he was nineteen, he enrolled in a philosophy course at a college in Jabalpur. A rebellious youth, he skipped classes and quarreled with his teachers. According to his own accounts, he went through a long period of spiritual crisis that ended one night with an explosive feeling of bliss and communion with the universe. It was the moment of enlightenment sought by innumerable mystics over the years. He was just twenty-one.

After graduating, Rajneesh was a university lecturer in philosophy for a while, but in 1960 he began traveling around India, expounding a philosophy of his own. He was a religious bowerbird, picking and choosing beliefs from Hinduism, Buddhism, Christianity, Jainism, Judaism, Tantra and the Western esoteric tradition. A major influence was the early twentieth-century Greek-Armenian mystic G. I. Gurdjieff, who believed that the main problem of modern life was that people were essentially asleep. Echoing Gurdjieff, Rajneesh proclaimed, 'I have come to wake you up.'

He gained a reputation as a brilliant orator in Hindi, and an iconoclast who made outrageous statements. He attacked other religions. He mocked Jainist precepts about chastity, and flaunted his own love of sex and cars. He even criticized Gandhi. Such behavior was, for most Indians, quite unbecoming in a guru, but they came in their thousands to hear him. In 1964, Rajneesh began to hold meditation camps. He experimented with a variety of techniques from around the world and, as the '60s wore on, was increasingly influenced by Western psychology and fashionable new techniques such as primal scream therapy and encounter groups.

Until now, Rajneesh had taught that people should spurn gurus and seek enlightenment within themselves, as he had done. In 1970, however, he began to initiate disciples. His first initiate was a Jain woman named Laxmi, who became his 'private secretary' and second-in-command, and was the first of his followers to wear exclusively orange clothes. This color was traditionally worn by wandering holy men, called sannyasins, who have renounced all worldly possessions. Orange clothes were soon adopted by Rajneesh's followers, who were also known as sannyasins; to the wider world, they were the Orange People. On initiation, he gave each of them a new name—usually incorporating the Hindi words for love (*prem*) or bliss (*anand*)—and a necklace of wooden beads with a locket containing his photograph.

The following year, Rajneesh gave himself a new name, 'Bhagwan,' which means 'the Blessed one,' while 'Shree' means 'revered.' A new god had arrived.

A GURU F⊕R THE TIⅢES

Rajneesh settled in Bombay (now Mumbai), and Western visitors to India began to seek him out. He was in many ways the perfect guru for the times. He encouraged his followers to have sex. He didn't care if they took drugs. He didn't care what they did, in fact, as long as they expressed their devotion to him and took part in the 'mad games' (as he described them) designed to break down their egos and get them to live in the present. They were captivated by his morning and evening talks, where he interspersed lofty discussions of the scriptures with dirty jokes. In a memoir about her time with Rajneesh, Rosemary Hamilton described the effect he had on his audience.

When he enters everything seems to part and make way for him, then fold itself around him. He turns slowly, palms together, to greet us, seeming to seek out the face of each one. Warm blood courses through my arms, hands, face. As he steps carefully to the podium I steal a glance around me. Every face is lit with joy as if a lamp

had been switched on inside. I know mine is alive with the same glow.

After initiation, sannyasins spent the next few months attending various ten-day group therapy sessions run by Rajneesh's lieutenants. Some of these were meditation groups but others were far more confrontational, designed to break down people's inhibitions, challenge their assumptions and force them to face their fears. Sometimes these groups got out of hand. Fights broke out and bones were broken, and some participants were made to face their fears literally. A person scared of snakes might be confronted with snakes; a woman who had been raped might be raped. Such practices proved too much for some, and there were several suicides.

Some Western converts became part of Rajneesh's inner circle. Others were sent home to spread the word, and the first Rajneesh Meditation Center outside India opened in London in 1971. The money Westerners brought in enabled the Rajneeshis to buy a 6-acre estate in the city of Poona (now Pune), on which they built an ashram. Over the next few years, the community grew until there were up to 6,000 there at any given time. With space in the ashram limited, most were forced to find accommodation in the city as best they could. Some supported themselves dealing drugs, while a few of the women worked as high-class prostitutes.

Rajneesh's sex life was the subject of much speculation among his followers. He often had private audiences, or 'darshans,' with female followers, and was known to boast of having had 'more women than any man in history.' He told his lovers that they were not to talk about their experiences, but from what some have revealed, it seems that his sex life consisted mainly of looking and touching.

95

While Rajneesh was all for sex, he had little time for children, and persuaded many converts to abandon theirs. He declared that the best thing for the world would be a two-year moratorium on childbirth. He urged his female followers to become sterilized and, to demonstrate their devotion to him, hundreds had tubal ligations. It was a decision many came to regret.

The community was thriving, but many in Poona resented the singing-and-dancing Westerners who had flooded their city. Conservative Indians were offended by their amorous behavior in public and the women's provocative dress (Rajneesh had encouraged them not to wear underwear as it interfered with 'the natural flow of energy'). Some sannyasins were attacked in the street, and a Hindu threw a knife at Rajneesh during one of his talks. Rajneesh instructed Laxmi to scour India for a suitable place for them to build their own city. But the Indian government had also turned against the group, revoking its tax-exempt status and blocking its attempts to buy land. Rajneesh turned to Laxmi's secretary, an Indian woman named Ma Anand Sheela, who had opened a Rajneeshi center in New Jersey in the early 1970s. She was in favor of moving to the United States, and Rajneesh eventually agreed. The official reason for going there was that he needed medical care for a bad back and other ailments.

After his departure, the community at Poona began to disperse. Millions of dollars were spirited out of the country. Sannyasins were instructed to apply for U.S. visas in groups of two or three so as not to arouse suspicion.

RANCHⴲ RAJNEESH

Sheela traveled through America looking for a suitable place to settle, and chose the 64,000-acre Big Muddy Ranch in Wasco County, Oregon, which was purchased for $5.75 million. The Rajneeshis threw a party for the local people on their arrival, and Sheela announced that all they wanted to do was set up a 'nice farm' with about forty workers. The locals were initially willing to give them the benefit of the doubt, but as hundreds of sannyasins clad in orange, pink and red began to arrive (they had now varied their color scheme somewhat), tensions inevitably mounted.

The sannyasins moved into trailers, and threw themselves into building their new community. The leisurely life they had enjoyed at Poona gave way to twelve-hour working days (although the word 'work' was banned, replaced by 'worship'). Urgent calls for donations went out to Rajneesh supporters around the world, and millions of dollars poured in. Hundreds of marriages were arranged between sannyasins to allow the non-U.S. citizens among them to stay in the country. In October 1981, the Rajneeshis applied to the Wasco County Court to have a portion of the ranch incorporated as a city, to be called Rajneeshpuram, and despite fierce opposition from the locals, the application was granted. They built a mall, restaurants, an airstrip, a reservoir and a meditation 'university.' They had their own newspaper and police force (the 'Peace Force'). By 1985, Rajneeshpuram had more than 2,500 permanent residents, with almost as many visitors there at any given time. The prodigious effort had paid off and the city began to make money.

Rajneesh had taken a vow of public silence before his arrival in America. He now spoke to his followers only through his inner circle, chiefly Ma Anand Sheela, who met with him every day. Sheela, who had total control over the day-to-day running of Rajneeshpuram, was a notoriously domineering, abrasive and short-tempered woman. Once, during a nationally televised debate on the *Nightline* program, her microphone was cut off after she repeatedly shouted 'Bullshit!' Another famous Sheela retort was 'Tough titties!', which she used several times in television interviews during a visit to Australia, where Rajneesh had many followers. It became a catchphrase across the country and is still remembered there today.

Rajneesh spent most of his time in his private quarters just outside the city, in a haze of Valium and nitrous oxide administered by his personal dentist. The only time most of his followers saw him was during his daily triumphal drive through Rajneeshpuram's main street in one of his Rolls-Royces. Rajneesh had acquired his first Rolls back in Poona, but in America his collection of them grew to a staggering ninety-three. When asked how their leader could possibly need these, the sannyasins usually replied that they loved Bhagwan, and wanted to make him happy, and he loved cars, so what was wrong with buying them for him? Rajneesh, of course, had never made a secret of his love of wealth and comfort. Yet, like so many of the things he said and did, the mad accumulation of Rolls-Royces seemed largely calculated to confuse both his enemies *and* his followers.

As Rajneeshpuram grew, there were constant challenges by locals to the Rajneeshis' land-use applications. Preachers declared Rajneesh the Antichrist. The immigration service was investigating the arranged marriages. Oregon's district attorney, Dave Frohnmayer, was putting together a case against the community based on the lack of separation between church and state in its administration. In turn, Rajneeshis made no attempt to disguise their contempt for the locals, and seemed to go out of their way to antagonize them.

In September 1984, more than 750 people in Wasco County's largest city, The Dalles, came down with salmonella poisoning, and forty-five were hospitalized. The outbreak was traced to food handlers in ten different restaurants. There was no apparent connection between the food handlers, however, and medical investigators were baffled.

P⊕IS⊕N AND PANIC

At this point, the Rajneeshis embarked on a bizarre plan to rig the upcoming elections for the Wasco County Court. Sannyasins fanned out across America, talking to homeless people and inviting them to start a new life in Rajneeshpuram. The 'Share-a-Home' program was, they maintained, purely altruistic. Oregonians quickly realized that its real purpose was to bring in enough voters to win the election and gain control over land use in the county.

Over several weeks, some 3,700 homeless people, mainly men, were taken by bus to Rajneeshpuram. Many were alcoholics, drugs addicts or mentally ill. The result was, predictably, chaos. The Rajneeshis found it impossible to control the newcomers, even though they had ordered in a large quantity of the powerful tranquillizer Haldol. Many were soon asked to leave. Realizing they would not have the numbers to achieve their goal, the Rajneeshis abandoned their plan and boycotted the election.

If there were outside pressures on Rajneesh's community, the forces most destructive to it were coming from within. There was a sense of mounting paranoia, with the streets patrolled by armed security guards, and visitors put under surveillance. When Rajneesh did his daily drive-through, a helicopter circled overhead, looking for snipers. The sexual freedom that had once been synonymous with the group had gone, too. Rajneesh, whose pronouncements had taken an increasingly apocalyptic tone, with warnings of impending natural disasters and nuclear war, had declared that AIDS would wipe out most of the world's population. Sannyasins were forbidden to have sex without condoms, or foreplay without surgical gloves, and when it was announced that AIDS could be transmitted through saliva, kissing was banned.

The most destructive element threatening the community, however, was Sheela. She and her female lieutenants, known as the 'moms,' lived in a house apart from the other sannyasins, in considerable luxury. Somehow, they seemed to know about everything that went on in the ranch. Anyone accused of being 'negative' was threatened with expulsion. Yet many sannyasins continued to believe that Rajneesh was guiding the community, and must know and approve of Sheela's actions.

Sheela finally overplayed her hand by turning on Rajneesh's inner circle, the only people on the ranch over whom she had no direct control. Rajneesh's long-time lover and chief companion, Vivek, fell ill after accepting a cup of tea from Sheela. She thought she had been poisoned, and told others of her suspicions, but no one could bring themselves to believe her. Then, Rajneesh's doctor, Deveraj, was stuck with a hypodermic needle by one of the 'moms,' Shanti Bhadra. He almost died. He had no doubt he had been poisoned, but some would not believe him either—even when he showed them the puncture wound on his buttock. For others, the attack on the doctor was a sobering event, and some long-standing sannyasins left the ranch.

Rajneeshpuram unraveled more quickly than anyone could have expected. Over two days in September 1985, Sheela and nineteen others left for Europe. On the morning of 16 September, Rajneesh (who had begun speaking in public again the year before) addressed his followers. Sheela, he told them, was a criminal who had tried to turn his community into 'a fascist concentration camp'. In addition to Vivek and Devaraj, Sheela and her coconspirators had poisoned several other sannyasins, and he hinted that they were also responsible for the salmonella outbreak. They had planted bugs and wiretaps throughout the ranch, and secretly dug tunnels beneath it—all of which was true. Rajneesh assured them that he had only just found out about it all, and was as shocked as anyone else.

The sannyasins were staggered by these revelations. They wanted to know why Rajneesh put a woman like Sheela in charge. 'I had chosen Sheela to give you a little taste of what fascism means,' he told them. The extent to which Rajneesh knew about Sheela's activities remains a matter for debate. Many are convinced that she was his pawn all along, her confrontational style merely an extension of his own.

Rajneesh invited the police to investigate his allegations and they were happy to oblige. They swarmed over the ranch, interviewed sannyasins and compiled a dossier of alleged crimes. Two Wasco County officers had been poisoned while visiting the community. Sheela's lieutenants had caused the salmonella poisonings by visiting the restaurants involved and contaminating food. These poisonings had actually been a dry run for the election—in addition to bringing in the homeless men, Sheela had planned to boost the Rajneeshis' chances by making many Oregonians too sick to vote. The police also found a 'death list' of intended victims, including the Oregonian and U.S. district attorneys, and hundreds of secretly taped conversations.

On 27 October, Rajneesh and six sannyasins were arrested in Charlotte, North Carolina, where they were about to board a plane bound for Bermuda. The following day, Sheela and two others were arrested in Germany and deported to the United States.

Rajneesh was charged on 35 felony counts, most of them relating to the arranged marriages, and spent twelve days in jail. He entered an 'Alford plea' on two charges (which means that, while not admitting guilt, he acknowledged that there was enough evidence to convict him). He was fined $400,000 and ordered to leave the country. Many at Rajneeshpuram wanted to stay on after his departure, but they soon realized that the community was not economically viable without Rajneesh as a drawcard. The ranch was sold and its assets dispersed.

In July 1986, Sheela was convicted of attempted murder, immigration fraud, wiretapping, food poisoning and various other crimes. She was sentenced to twenty years in prison, but was paroled after two and a half years. Upon her release, she went to Switzerland, where she set up two homes for the mentally disabled, with which she is still involved.

Following his departure from the United States, Rajneesh went on a 'world tour,' which mainly consisted of him being thrown out of some countries (Crete and Uruguay) and barred from entering others. He eventually returned to India. In 1989, he gave himself a new name—Osho, a play on the phrase 'oceanic feeling' that William James used to describe religious experience. He died the following year, claiming at the end that he had been given a slow-acting poison by the U.S. government during his brief stint of imprisonment. His ashes are kept at the ashram in Pune, which remains a popular spot for spiritual pilgrims. Each night they watch on a huge screen one of 5,000 of the master's discourses that were videotaped in his lifetime. His epitaph is 'OSHO. Never Born, Never Died. Only Visited this Planet Earth between Dec 11 1931–Jan 19 1990.'

Charlie's PE⊕PLE

The Manson Family

(Founded 1967)

I play faces for the clowns, but the real me is a rattlesnake, a wolf, a scorpion, nothing ... I'm ... at war with lies, pollution, confusion, and fools who've got no intelligence.

Charles Manson

ON THE MORNING OF 9 AUGUST 1969, WINIFRED CHAPMAN, the housekeeper at 10050 Cielo Drive, Beverly Hills, let herself in through the service entrance at the back. Walking through the kitchen into the living room, she saw blood, in pools on the floor and splashes on the walls, blood everywhere, and, glancing through the open front door, a body on the lawn. As she ran to the house next door to raise the alarm, she passed a car in the driveway and saw another body inside it.

The house was being rented by the Polish-born film director Roman Polanski and his actress wife, Sharon Tate. Polanski was working in Europe at the time. While he was away, their friends Wojciech Frykowski and his common-law wife Abigail Folger, a coffee heiress, had been staying with Tate. Another friend, celebrity hairstylist Jay Sebring, had come to visit the previous night.

Police arrived and searched the house and grounds. The bodies of Frykowski and Folger were found on the lawn; those of Sebring and Tate—who had been eight and a half months pregnant—were in the living room. All had been stabbed many times. The body in the car belonged to Steven Parent, a friend of the house's caretaker. He had been shot. Someone had scrawled the word 'PIG' on the front door in blood.

The following night, supermarket executive Leno LaBianca and his wife Rosemary were stabbed to death in their home in Los Feliz, Los Angeles. The words 'RISE' and 'DEATH TO PIGS' were written in blood on the walls, while 'HEALTER SKELTER' [sic] was found on the refrigerator.

The Los Angeles Police Department, in charge of the Tate murder investigation, initially refused to see any link between the two cases. The Los Angeles Sheriff's Office, handling the LaBianca case, believed they *were* linked, and also saw similarities to the murder of a musician, Bobby Hinman, which had taken place in July. A man named Bobby Beausoleil had already been arrested and charged with Hinman's murder. Beausoleil had been a member of a group known as the Family, led by a thirty-four-year-old ex-con named Charles Manson.

'A TEXT B⊕⊕K INSTITUTI⊕NAL INⅢATE'

Manson was born on 12 November 1934 in Cincinnati, Ohio, the illegitimate son of sixteen-year-old Kathleen Maddox and a 'Colonel Scott' from Kentucky. He acquired his surname when Kathleen was briefly married to a much older man named William Manson.

Kathleen may not have been a prostitute, as Manson later claimed, but she was promiscuous and an alcoholic, and thought nothing of abandoning her son for months at a time. There is a story that she once sold him to a waitress for a pitcher of beer (his uncle later retrieved him). Manson spent most of his early years in the care of his strictly religious aunt and uncle.

When he was twelve, Kathleen tried to have him fostered out, and he ended up in a boys' home in Indiana. It was the first of a long list of institutions he would inhabit over the next two decades. He began his life of crime by breaking into stores, and at thirteen committed his first armed robbery. Reports by various case workers and psychiatrists over the years paint a picture of an antisocial boy, insecure because of his short stature and emotionally crippled by his mother's rejection. He was also highly intelligent and a skilful manipulator of others.

In 1952, while in a minimum security facility, Manson held a razor blade to another boy's throat and raped him. He was transferred to the Federal Reformatory at

Petersburg, Virginia, and paroled in 1954. He married a waitress named Rosalie Willis, who became pregnant. When Manson missed a court hearing, his parole was revoked and he was sentenced to three years' jail. Rosalie divorced him, winning custody of their son, Charles, Jr.

Prison authorities remained pessimistic about Manson's chances for rehabilitation, with one report calling him 'an almost classic text book case of the correctional institutional inmate.' Nevertheless, he was granted parole again in 1958. He began a new career as a pimp, and married a prostitute, who bore him another son. He got another girl pregnant (after conning $700 from her) and drugged and raped her flatmate. He was caught trying to cash a forged cheque. Manson was eventually sent back to jail, this time to the federal penitentiary at McNeil Island, Washington, to finish the ten-year sentence he had been previously serving. He shared a cell with Alvin Karpis, the famed 1930s bank robber, who taught him how to play guitar. Manson had dreams of becoming a rock star. He wrote dozens of songs, and told people he was going to be bigger than the Beatles.

For a while, Manson was a keen Scientologist. He read the Bible, committing many passages to memory. He devoured books on psychotherapy, hypnotism and black magic. It seems that, if the rock star dream didn't pan out, Manson was planning another career to fall back on.

Manson was released from prison in March 1967. Legend has it that, at the last minute, he begged the authorities to let him stay. They refused, and Charles Manson, who had spent seventeen of his thirty-two years in institutions, was ejected into the outside world.

THE CREEPY CRAWLERS

Manson roamed the streets of Los Angeles, playing his guitar and begging. He met Mary Brunner, a twenty-three-year-old librarian at the University of California, moved into her apartment, and persuaded her to let other girls move in too. The Family began to grow. Its members would always be predominately female, despite the fact that Manson thought women were good for only two things—serving men and having babies. Many of the women who joined were estranged from their real families, and Manson was adept at picking their fears and weaknesses. He loved to break down their inhibitions, plying them with drugs and introducing them to group sex.

Manson said that his job was to 'unprogram' people, to erase their egos and rid them of everything they had learnt from parents, schools, government. He taught that life and death were illusions, that all actions were permissible, that the important thing was to be self-aware and live in the 'now.' Fear was good, because a person who was afraid was the most self-aware of all. Anyone who questioned Manson too closely about these ideas was discouraged. 'No sense makes sense,' he liked to say.

More important than his philosophy was Manson's personality, which many found hypnotic. He was often compared to a chameleon, his face and moods constantly changing. His followers believed that he had supernatural powers. Some thought he could read their thoughts and see what they were doing wherever they were.

After a period in San Francisco, Manson and about ten followers, including Susan Atkins, Lynette 'Squeaky' Fromme and Patricia Krenwinkel, went on the road in an old yellow school bus painted black. They survived by doing odd jobs, begging, petty theft and raiding the bins outside supermarkets for discarded food. They broke into

109

houses, but not just to steal. They liked to creep around in the dark as the occupants slept, moving furniture and other objects. They called it 'creepy crawling.'

In 1968, two of Manson's female followers were hitchhiking in Malibu when they were picked up by Dennis Wilson from the Beach Boys, who took them to his sprawling rock-star residence. Manson was keen to establish contacts in the music industry, and the Family moved into Wilson's house. Wilson was happy to have them there—for a while at least. He was interested in Manson's philosophy and thought he had real musical talent. (One of his songs, 'Cease to Exist,' renamed 'Never Learn Not to Love,' appeared on the Beach Boys' 1969 album *20/20*.) Wilson introduced him to Terry Melcher, a record producer and the son of Doris Day. Manson was desperate to make an album, but after listening to two of his performances, Melcher declined to take him on. Melcher was living at 10050 Cielo Drive at the time.

Dennis Wilson eventually tired of Manson's sponging, and had the group evicted from his house in August 1968. They went to live on the Spahn Movie Ranch, a 500-acre property in the Santa Susana Mountains. It had a replica Western town that had often been used for movies and TV programs, but its main business now was renting horses. It was owned by eighty-one-year-old, almost blind, George Spahn. Manson had Squeaky Fromme move into his trailer, where she cooked for him, slept with him, and ensured that he knew little about the Family's activities on his property.

From late 1968, a number of murders took place in California that remain unsolved, but which some believe were committed by members of the Family. Their first undoubted victim was Gary Hinman, an easy-going music teacher with an interest in Buddhism, who had

110

often let members of the Family stay at his house in Topanga Canyon.

On 25 July 1969, Bobby Beausoleil, a charismatic, good-looking musician who was nicknamed 'Cupid,' arrived at Hinman's house accompanied by Susan Atkins and Mary Brunner. As the story is usually told, Hinman had sold some inferior mescaline to the Straight Satans, a motorcycle gang whose members hung around the Spahn Ranch (chiefly because of the women there), and Beausoleil had been sent to get their money back. According to another version, Manson had simply heard that Hinman had come into money, and sent Beausoleil to get it. Whatever the reason for the visit, when Hinman wouldn't produce any money, Beausoleil pistol-whipped him. He rang the ranch for further instructions, and Manson and another follower, Bruce Davis, came over.

Hinman begged them to leave him alone. Manson, who had brought a sword with him, responded by striking Hinman in the head with it, slicing his left ear in two. He and Davis left, and Beausoleil continued to pressure Hinman for money, which he insisted he didn't have. After three days of torture, Beausoleil gave up and stabbed Hinman to death. Before he and the women left the house, he wrote 'POLITICAL PIGGIES' on the wall in blood.

HELTER SKELTER

Manson said that his philosophy was all about love, but when it came to the apocalyptic scenario he had pieced together by the beginning of 1969, what he hated loomed larger. In particular, Manson hated authority in all its forms—the 'pigs'—and black people, whom he considered inferior to whites. He told his followers that a race war was imminent, which he called 'Helter Skelter' after the raucous song on the Beatles' just released 'White Album.' (Manson believed that the Beatles were prophets, and identified them as the four angels mentioned in the Book of Revelation.) It would begin with blacks invading the homes of whites, savagely murdering them, and writing messages in their blood. An epic conflict between black and white would follow, which the blacks would win, killing all the whites except Manson and his followers. They would take refuge from the carnage in a hidden city beneath Death Valley that could be entered through a hole in the ground. Though the blacks would triumph, they would be incapable of running the world. Manson and his followers, their number now grown to 144,000 (a figure derived from the Book of Revelation), would emerge from underground to take over, and Manson would rule the world.

Most of Manson's followers believed it all. Some even searched for the hole.

There was only one problem. Manson was sure that Helter Skelter would begin in 1969, but as the months went by, there was still no sign of it. Increasingly frustrated, he told his followers, 'The only thing black knows is what whitie has told him. *I'm* going to have to show him how to do it.'

On the evening of 8 August, Manson took Charles 'Tex' Watson aside. Watson, who was born in Dallas, Texas, had been a football-playing, church-going honors student, but drink and drugs had taken their toll, and he had become one of Manson's most ardent followers. Manson gave him a gun and a knife and ordered him to go to 10050 Cielo Drive and kill everyone there. Manson knew that Terry Melcher no longer lived there. Having visited the house once while looking for him, he also knew that it was isolated. Watson had been inside the house several times, so he knew the layout.

Manson told Susan Atkins, Patricia Krenwinkel and Linda Kasabian to go with Watson. Kasabian had only been a member of the Family for about a month, and it seems he chose her because she had a current driver's licence. The women were armed with knives and, before they left, Manson instructed them to leave writing at the scene.

They arrived at the house just after midnight. Watson climbed the telephone pole and cut the wires. He and the women had just made it over the security fence when a car came down the driveway. It was driven by eighteen-year-old Steven Parent, who had been visiting the house's caretaker, William Garretson, who lived in a guesthouse at the back. Watson went up to the car. Parent said, 'Please don't hurt me. I won't say anything.' Watson shot him four times.

Watson cut a window screen, climbed in, and let Atkins and Krenwinkel in through the front door. (He had told Kasabian to keep watch outside.) In the living room, they came upon Wojciech Frykowski asleep on a couch. Watson pointed the gun at his head and woke him. When Frykowski asked who he was, Watson replied, 'I am the devil and I've come to do the devil's business.'

Watson told Atkins to tie Frykowski's hands, then see who else was in the house. Walking down the hallway, she saw Abigail Folger in a bedroom reading a book. She smiled and waved at Folger, who smiled and waved back. In the next bedroom she saw the heavily pregnant Sharon Tate lying on a bed, talking to Jay Sebring. When she reported back, Watson told her and Krenwinkel to bring all three into the living room.

Watson ordered the hostages to lie on their stomachs on the floor. 'Can't you see she's pregnant?' said Sebring. 'Let her sit down!' Watson shot him.

He asked if they had any money, and Folger gave Atkins the cash from her purse. Watson used a nylon rope he had brought with him to tie Tate, Folger and Sebring together by their necks. He told Atkins to kill Frykowski, but as she had her knife raised, Frykowski managed to free his hands. They began to struggle, with Frykowski pulling her hair and Atkins stabbing at him blindly. Frykowski broke away and ran for the front door, pursued by Watson, who caught up with him, bashed his head with the gun so hard the butt broke, then stabbed him repeatedly. He then went to help Krenwinkel with Abigail Folger, who had also escaped onto the lawn.

That left Sharon Tate, still tied up in the living room. She pleaded for her life and the life of her unborn baby. Susan Atkins said, 'Woman, I have no mercy for you,' and stabbed her to death.

Before they left, Watson remembered they were supposed to write something. Atkins dipped a towel in Sharon Tate's blood and wrote 'PIGS.'

Helter Skelter continued the following night. This time, Watson, Atkins, Krenwinkel and Kasabian were joined by 'Clem' Grogan, Leslie Van Houten and Manson who, having been told how messy the previous night was, said he could do better. After driving around for a while, they stopped outside the LaBiancas' house. Manson went inside, then returned saying he had pacified the two occupants and tied them up. He sent Watson, Atkins and Van Houten in. Watson killed Leno LaBianca, while both the women stabbed Rosemary. Leno was left with a knife in his throat, a fork sticking out of his stomach, and the word 'WAR' carved into his chest.

The extraordinarily vicious nature of the murders at the Tate house (Frykowski had been hit on the head thirteen times, stabbed fifty-one times and shot twice) was sensational enough, but the LaBianca killings, following so soon after, sent real panic throughout the Los Angeles area. In the first few weeks, the police investigation got nowhere. The refusal of the Los Angeles Police Department, who believed the Tate murders were the result of a drug deal gone wrong, to see any connection with the LaBianca case seems incomprehensible in hindsight. But the Family would soon give themselves away.

Less than a week after the Tate murders, police raided the Spahn Ranch and arrested Manson and many of his followers on car theft and arson charges. Although most were soon released, they were re-arrested at a second raid in October, this time at a ranch near Death Valley. In jail, Susan Atkins confessed in horrifying detail to two other inmates her role in the Tate killings. She described how she had tasted Sharon Tate's blood after killing her— 'Wow, what a trip!'—and considered cutting her baby out before deciding there wasn't enough time.

In November, during an interview with the Los Angeles Sheriff's Office, a member of the Straight Satans named Al Springer described being at Spahn Ranch two or three days after the Tate murders. Manson, bragging about killing, had told him, 'We knocked off five of them just the other night.'

X-ING ⲺUT

The trial of Charles Manson, Susan Atkins, Patricia Krenwinkel and Leslie Van Houton began on 24 July 1970. (Friends in high places had stalled the extradition of Tex Watson from Texas, and he had to be tried later.) Manson entered the courtroom with an 'X' carved on his forehead. Outside, Squeaky Fromme and some of the other Manson girls (they would maintain a vigil throughout the trial) handed out copies of a statement by Manson. It read in part:

I have X-ed myself from your world ... My faith in me is stronger than all of your armies, governments, gas chambers, or anything you may want to do to me. I know what I have done. Your courtroom is a man's game. Love is my judge.

The prosecutor was LA's deputy district attorney, Vincent Bugliosi. His most important witness was Linda Kasabian. She had not actively participated in any of the killings and had since shown great remorse for them (unlike the other three women, who showed no remorse at all). She had been granted immunity from prosecution as long as she told everything she knew. Bugliosi introduced physical evidence to connect Watson and the women with the murders, but he was also determined that Manson, as the mastermind, should receive the death penalty. He had a difficult task here. Manson was not present at Cielo Drive, or when the LaBiancas were killed, and the idea that the motive for seven supremely callous murders was to trigger a race war seemed so preposterous that few other lawyers believed a jury would accept it. However, Bugliosi was able to call upon numerous witnesses who had heard Manson talk about Helter Skelter, and built a meticulous case. He was helped by the behavior of the defendants throughout the trial, with Manson making threats and the women obviously under his control.

Manson had asked if he could defend himself, and was furious when the court imposed an attorney on him.

It was clear that he wanted a joint defence with the women, which would allow them to testify that he had not ordered the killings. (They did in fact do this during the sentencing part of the trial.) This caused a great deal of tension between the women and their attorneys, who were trying to do their best for them. In the middle of the trial, Ronald Hughes, the attorney defending Leslie Van Houten, mysteriously disappeared. Bugliosi wasn't the only one who thought the Family had murdered him. (Hughes' decomposed body was later found in Ventura County, but no cause of death was ever established.)

On 25 January 1971, after six months of harrowing testimony and theatrics from the defendants, the jury handed down their verdicts, finding all four guilty of first-degree murder. All were sentenced to death. Later that year, Bugliosi prosecuted Tex Watson, and he too was sentenced to death, as was Bobby Beausoleil after two trials. In 1972, when capital punishment was briefly declared unconstitutional in California, all the death sentences were commuted to life imprisonment.

In 1975, Squeaky Fromme, who had continued to be the chief promoter of Manson's message (now mutated into an environmental one) pulled a gun on President Gerald Ford. She was sentenced to life imprisonment.

All of the killers remain in prison. They regularly seek parole, and perhaps it will eventually be granted to some of them. Manson, however, will never be released. With his notoriety as strong as ever, he remains a poster boy for nihilistic rebellion. His songs are regularly covered by rock bands. He receives thousands of letters yearly. Should he ever see the light of day, he could gather a cult that would dwarf his ramshackle crew of 1969.

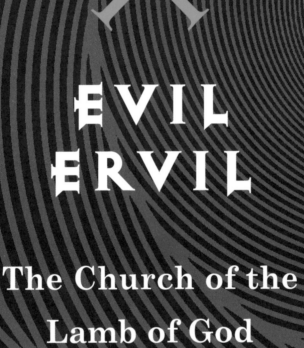

EVIL ERVIL

The Church of the
Lamb of God
(Founded 1972)

The Kingdom of God must exist by force.

Ervil LeBaron

THE VENGEFUL GOD OF THE OLD TESTAMENT was Ervil LeBaron's God of choice. He was a fundamentalist Mormon of the most pure kind, his beliefs simplified down to a single proposition: the Ten Commandments are the word of the Lord, and the sentence for breaking them is death. Only when this is accepted will the Kingdom of God come to pass.

Yet, for all the scriptural arguments he could muster, most people just couldn't see it his way. So he went to war. His brother, and rival for religious leadership, was the first casualty. Later, his pregnant daughter would lie among the dead. And even after his own death in a Utah prison cell, many more would be killed on the orders of Ervil LeBaron.

A FAMILY OF PROPHETS

In 1831, the founder of the Church of Jesus Christ of Latter Day Saints, Joseph Smith, Jr., received a revelation that righteous men should take more than one wife. Polygamy, or plural marriage, became a feature of Mormon life, at first practiced secretly, then publicly acknowledged by Smith's successor, Brigham Young. It led to decades of persecution for the sect, which largely ceased when the practice was officially discontinued in 1890. Polygamy was later made an offence punishable by excommunication, but a small number of Mormons, known as fundamentalists, have continued to practice it.

In 1923, a devout Mormon named Dayer LeBaron was living with his wife, Maud, and eight children in the tiny town of La Verkin, Utah. Dayer and Maud had long been contemplating plural marriage, and it was she who chose a girl eighteen years Dayer's junior to be his second wife. When word got around that he had married her, Dayer and Maud were excommunicated and he was threatened with arrest. The family fled to Mexico.

Mexico had long been a refuge for polygamist Mormons. Dayer had, in fact, lived there years before, when his father also planned on taking a second wife (as it happened, she never showed up for the wedding). Dayer took his family to the same place, a Mormon community called Colonia Juarez. Shortly after their arrival, on 22 February 1925, Maud gave birth to a ninth child. He was named Ervil.

Unfortunately for the LeBarons, the Mormons in Colonia Juarez had turned against polygamy. Other church members were forbidden from visiting their home, and the children were bullied in the streets. Nevertheless, they still considered themselves to be true Mormons, and during the early 1940s, Ervil and two of his brothers, Joel and Alma, briefly hit the road as missionaries.

The LeBaron boys thought they were made for better things, though. Their grandfather, Benjamin Johnson, had been a staunch polygamist and close friend of Joseph Smith. There was a family story that, before his death in 1905, Johnson had taken Dayer aside. He revealed that Joseph Smith had bestowed upon him 'authority over the earth,' and passed this on to Dayer. While Dayer had never been inclined to exercise this authority, his sons were different. The eldest, Benjamin, received revelations from an early age, and believed he was the last prophet, 'The One Mighty and Strong,' foretold in scripture. Alma and Ervil became his first followers, and when they embraced the doctrine of polygamy, all three were excommunicated. Benjamin's behavior became increasingly erratic, and he was diagnosed with schizophrenia. He spent the rest of his life in and out of mental institutions.

In 1944, Dayer moved the family to an even more isolated place in the desert, near Galeana, Chihuahua, which he named Colonia LeBaron. Dayer, Maud and various combinations of their twelve children scratched a living growing fruit there, occasionally joined by polygamists on the lam from the United States.

Dayer died in 1951. Joel claimed that before he died, his father laid hands on him and passed on the 'authority' given to him by Benjamin Johnson. In 1955 Joel started his own church—the Church of the Firstborn of the Fulness [sic] of Time. He issued a revelation calling on other fundamentalists to relocate to Colonia LeBaron, which he called the 'Land of Zion.' The other LeBarons were sceptical about Joel's prophetic claims, but eventually most of them came around. Ervil, given the title of 'Patriarch,' became Joel's second-in-command.

ZI⊕N IN THE DESERT

Life was hard, dusty and flyblown among the adobe huts of Colonia LeBaron. There was no electricity or running water, and food was in short supply. Nevertheless, a community began to take shape. In 1959, about one hundred people turned up for the biannual conference.

Aside from their fundamentalist beliefs, Joel and Ervil could not have been more different. Joel was a deeply religious man who was loved by his followers. Ervil, though respected for his scriptural knowledge, was a hard man to like. Joel wore his fundamentalism lightly, but once Ervil started talking scripture, he could go for hours on end. Joel didn't mind getting his hands dirty working in the colony's fields and orchards, but Ervil never did a scrap of work. More than anything else, Joel avoided conflict while Ervil relished it.

Ervil believed that his role as Patriarch entitled him to many wives. The official tally eventually rose to thirteen, although there may have been more. After taking two Mexican brides in the mid-1950s, he enticed Anna Mae Marston away from her husband, who was one of the original Firstborners (causing a scandal). His fourth wife was an eighteen-year-old blonde beauty named Lorna Chynoweth. Lorna's mother, Thelma, had brought her husband, Bud, and five of their children into the fold. Later, Lorna's younger sister Rena became Ervil's thirteenth wife. He married another girl, Kristina Jensen, when she was fourteen.

Ervil also acted as the church's unofficial marriage broker—despite Joel's objections that people should be free to marry whomever they wanted—and enjoyed the power it brought. Later, he would use his own daughters as bargaining chips.

Ervil's religious views became more extreme. He developed the doctrine of 'Civil Law,' which basically meant the death penalty for anyone who broke the Ten Commandments. He became an obsessive writer, shutting himself in his room for days as he composed sulphurous paragraphs, neglecting to bathe or shave, fueled by coffee that made his notoriously bad breath even worse. In pamphlet after pamphlet he railed against the Mormon church and other fundamentalist groups. He alarmed the women with talk of enemies being beheaded and disemboweled, and asked the men if they were willing to kill for the Lord. In his more grandiose moments, he spoke of overthrowing the U.S. government and installing a Firstborner in the White House. When some expressed their concerns about Ervil's ravings to Joel, he brushed them aside.

In 1964, after receiving a revelation, Joel began to buy up beachfront property in Baja California. He wanted to create a cooperative where poor people could live and work. About 200 eventually settled at Los Molinos, as the community was called. Ervil belatedly realized the potential the land had for a resort. Having never made a secret of his desire to grow rich, he had embarked on several businesses that had failed dismally. He saw that selling Los Molinos to developers could reap millions, but Joel stuck to his original vision for the land. Tensions between the two brothers mounted.

In October 1970, after hearing that Ervil was talking about deposing him, Joel announced that he would be replaced as Patriarch by his brother Verlan. Ervil accepted his demotion graciously in public, but privately he was furious. In May 1971 he founded his own church, the Church of the Lamb of God, in San Diego. A number of the Firstborners followed him there, including Dan Jordan, who had been his right-hand man for years. Jordan, known for his cold manner and blinking black eyes, had helped Ervil put together the doctrine of 'Civil Law.'

In August 1971, a twenty-eight-page document entitled *Message to a Covenant People* appeared. Written by Ervil and Jordan, it called Joel's failure to recognize Ervil's authority 'an act of treason against heaven that carries the penalty of death in this world.' Joel reacted with fatalism. When one of Verlan's wives asked Joel how far he thought Ervil's followers would go, he looked at her and replied, 'I will be killed.'

On Sunday, 20 August, Joel dropped by the house of Bejamin Zarate in Ensenada. Zarate and his family had gone over to Ervil, but Joel remained on good terms with them. Another Ervil follower named Gamaliel Rios was also there, and a few minutes later, Dan Jordan arrived.

Joel's fourteen-year-old son Ivan, who was waiting outside, heard the sounds of a fight, then two shots. He ran in to find his father lying dead on the floor, bullet wounds in his throat and head.

Ervil seems to have thought that with Joel dead, the Church of the Firstborn would simply fall into his hands. However, most of the Firstborners backed Verlan, who became president. The Mexican police issued a wanted poster with photos of Ervil, Dan Jordan, Gamaliel Rios and four others, but most of them had fled to the United States. The FBI was alerted, but agents assigned to the case could make little sense of this war among polygamists.

In December 1972, Ervil LeBaron surprised everybody by walking into a Mexican police station accompanied by two lawyers and demanding that the charges against him be dropped. He was arrested and put on trial the following year, but the case was hampered by the absence of Jordan and Rios. LeBaron was found guilty, but the verdict was later overturned—the Firstborners suspected bribery—and he was released after spending fourteen months in jail.

'JUDGEMENTS AND DESTRUCTIONS'

In May 1974, LeBaron issued another pamphlet designed to curdle the blood of the Firstborners. *Hour of Crisis—Day of Vengeance*, featuring a hand holding a sword on its cover, threatened that all those who did not heed the word of God's messenger (that is, Ervil) 'would be destroyed from off the face of the earth through the pouring out of judgements and destructions.'

Just after 9 p.m. on 26 December, a pickup truck drove into Los Molinos. The men inside it had shotguns, revolvers and Molotov cocktails. It was followed by a car driven by sixteen-year-old Rena Chynoweth. She was accompanied by three of LeBaron's sons, who had been promised some 'fireworks.'

The truck drove up to a three-storey house, the largest in the community. Molotov cocktails were hurled and it burst into flames. Residents came running and made frantic efforts to douse the fire, some climbing onto the roof. They had just about succeeded when a volley of shots rang out. The assailants got back in their truck and drove off, throwing more firebombs as they went, heading for Verlan's house. They shot through its windows and pelted it with firebombs. Verlan wasn't there, though, and his wife and children were able to get out in time.

Two young Mexican boys were killed in the raid, thirteen people were wounded and seven buildings destroyed.

Shortly after this, another murder took place. Noemi Zarate, one of the wives of Bud Chynoweth, had grown disenchanted with the group and threatened to go to the police. She disappeared in January 1975, and her body was never found. While no one was ever charged with the murder, the police were later told that Noemi was killed by Ervil's wife, Vonda White.

The next to face LeBaron's wrath was a Mormon named Robert Simons. After suffering a nervous breakdown, Simons had come to believe he was a prophet with a mission to lead the Native Americans to 'the Latter Days.' One day, a friend gave him a Lamb of God flier to read, and he was intrigued enough to write to them. LeBaron and Dan Jordan turned up at his ranch in Grantsville, Utah. They gave false names (and Jordan was wearing a wig). During this and subsequent visits, LeBaron did his best to recruit Simons. It seems their meetings got a little wild, with the two self-styled prophets speaking in tongues and writhing about on the floor. Simons remained unswayed by Ervil's arguments, and when LeBaron started to show an interest in one of his wives, wrote a letter challenging his authority. That was too much for LeBaron, who said that the Lord had ordered Simons' death.

Lloyd Sullivan, who had joined the Lambs just before the Los Molinos raid, had become one of LeBaron's most trusted lieutenants. On 21 April 1975, he went to Simons' ranch. He had been there before with LeBaron, and gotten on well with Simons and his family. Sullivan now said that he had fallen out with LeBaron. He also said that he had spoken to some Native American leaders about Simons being their 'white prophet,' and wanted to arrange a meeting between them. Simons was enthusiastic.

Sullivan returned two nights later to take Simons to the meeting. After driving for three hours, they arrived at a remote spot in the desert marked with a pile of stones. Mark Chynoweth and Eddie Marston (the son of Ervil's third wife, Anna Mae) were waiting. When Simons got out of the car, Marston shot him in the back of the head. He was buried in a grave dug earlier in solid rock.

LeBaron threatened those who betrayed him with 'hot lead and cold steel' or 'a one-way ticket to hell.' It seems that the next murder was committed to reinforce the point. Dean Vest was a tall, bearded Vietnam veteran whose father had been a Firstborner. At a loose end after the war ended, he hooked up with the Lambs of God, and helped plan the Los Molinos raid. His wife hated Ervil, though, and when LeBaron heard that Vest had agreed to leave, decreed a 'blood atonement' killing and assigned Vonda White to the task. On June 12, Vest dropped by White's house in San Diego. He was washing

127

his hands at the kitchen sink when she shot him twice in the back. She told the police that she had been upstairs when the shooting took place, and suggested the Church of the Firstborn had done it.

'I WONDER IF REBECCA'S IN THE TRUNK'

With the Utah police asking questions about Robert Simons' disappearance, Ervil moved operations to Denver. The Lambs of God began a business refurbishing and selling old washing machines and other appliances. Victor Chynoweth, the most commercially savvy of the group, started an auto salvage business.

In March 1976, LeBaron was spotted in Mexico by a Firstborner, who alerted police. He was arrested and put on trial for his involvement in the Los Molinos raid, but the judge eventually threw out the charges. Again, bribery was suspected.

After his release from jail, LeBaron and some of his followers moved to Dallas, where they started another appliance business. His teenage daughter Rebecca also moved there. She had married one of the Chynoweth boys, Victor, but their relationship had soured. Rebecca, who was pregnant with her second child, was known to be mentally unstable, and began threatening to go to the police.

In April 1977, Lloyd Sullivan was in the group's Dallas warehouse when he noticed that LeBaron's car was sagging at the back. 'I wonder if Rebecca's in the trunk,' said Ervil airily. Sullivan opened it and saw Rebecca's body curled up inside. Lloyd's son, Don, later told police that Eddie Marston had strangled her and buried her body in the desert. It has never been found.

DEATH ⊕F A NATUR⊕PATH

The Lambs of God were doing well from their various businesses, but their movement had stalled. Selling secondhand washing machines was a far cry from taking over the Mormon church, or indeed the U.S. government. LeBaron also had a problem of his own making, having prophesied that a momentous event would take place by May 1977. Though the details were vague, the implication was that their chief enemy, the Church of the Firstborn, would be destroyed by then. LeBaron knew that something dramatic needed to be done if he was to retain his prophetic status.

On 20 April, LeBaron held a meeting of about twenty-five followers in Dallas. He told them that Rulon Allred, the leader of the polygamist Mormon sect the United Apostolic Brethren, was to be killed. Two women would carry this out—his latest wife, Rena Chynoweth, and Dan Jordan's wife (and Eddie Marston's sister) Ramona.

Rulon Allred and the LeBarons went back a long way. When Dayer founded Colonia LeBaron in the 1940s, Allred was one of the first American polygamists to seek sanctuary there. Later, when Joel declared himself a prophet, the revelation he issued calling for other fundamentalists to join him had been addressed to Allred. Ervil had issued further demands to Allred and his group over the years, all of which had been ignored. By 1977, the Apostolic Brethren had some 2000 members, and were fabulously wealthy compared with Ervil's ramshackle Lambs of God.

The murder of Allred was only the first part of the plan. Ervil was sure that his elusive brother Verlan would attend Allred's funeral. (Following Joel's murder, Verlan had wisely kept on the move, spending much of his time in the United States and Nicaragua.) The funeral

129

would provide the opportunity for a second team, led by the group's 'military leader,' Don Sullivan, to despatch the false prophet. Ervil was certain of success, having watched the whole scenario play out in a vision.

Allred, aged seventy-one, was a naturopath with a clinic on the outskirts of Salt Lake City. At about 4.45 p.m. on 10 May, Rena and Ramona, wearing wigs, entered the clinic. Allred, who had been attending to a patient, walked past them into the diagnostic room. Rena followed him in and, pointing a gun at him, fired seven times. Hearing the shots and Allred's screams, Melba, one of his eight wives who also worked as his secretary, came running and found him on his back, blood spurting from his chest. Rena and Ramona ran out. Allred's friend, Richard Bunker, who had been in the reception area, went to the door, hoping to get the registration number of a getaway car. He was horrified to see them coming back. There was a scuffle and Bunker had a gun put to his head, but he broke away and locked himself in the restroom. Rena returned to where the naturopath lay bleeding and fired a last shot at his head, which missed.

On 14 May, Dan Sullivan, Eddie Marston and a recent recruit to the cause, Jack Strothman, were in a pickup truck heading for Rulon Allred's funeral. They were armed with automatic rifles and numerous rounds of ammunition. As they approached the venue, they didn't like what they saw. According to LeBaron's vision, the funeral was supposed to take place in the open. Instead, it was in a high school, and there were police and television camera crews swarming all over it. It was left to the 'military leader' to make the call. 'No way,' Sullivan told the other two. 'This is stupid. We're not gonna do nothin'.'

LeBaron's group were obvious suspects for Allred's murder, and the police determined that one of the guns used in the attack had been purchased by Victor Chynoweth's wife Nancy. She was arrested on 22 May, and further arrests followed. The police's biggest coup came with the arrest of Lloyd and Don Sullivan. Lloyd, who had become thoroughly disillusioned with LeBaron, told them everything he knew. He gave them details of the murders of Noemi Zarate, Dean Vest, Robert Simons and Rebecca LeBaron. He also led them to Simons' desert grave.

Lloyd Sullivan testified at the preliminary hearing against Vonda White for the murder of Dean Vest, but died of a heart attack a month later. The loss of the prosecution's star witness was sorely felt at the Allred murder trial, which began on 6 March 1979. Of those accused of murder, Rena, Mark and Victor Chynoweth and Eddie Marston were present in the court, while Ervil LeBaron was at large in Mexico and Ramona Marston had skipped bail and disappeared. Don Sullivan gave evidence for the prosecution, but was tainted as a witness by his involvement in the conspiracy to kill Verlan. The prosecution had other problems. They could place all of the accused in Salt Lake City at the time of the murder, but physical evidence linking them to it was lacking, and the two witnesses to the killing, Melba Allred and Richard Bunker, could not identify Rena as the gunwoman. In the end, the four defendants were acquitted. (In her 1990 book *The Blood Covenant*, Rena admitted shooting Rulon Allred. Ramona Marston gave herself up in 1981, entered a plea bargain, and was sentenced to two years' probation.) After an aborted first trial, Vonda White was sentenced to life imprisonment.

In May 1979, the Mexican police got around to arresting LeBaron and, after roughing him up, handed him over to the FBI. He went on trial on 12 May 1980, charged with the first-degree murder of Rulon Allred and conspiracy to murder Verlan LeBaron. Don Sullivan and Ervil's son Isaac gave evidence against him. On 28 May, the jury found him guilty on both counts. LeBaron was sentenced to life imprisonment.

In jail, learning that the many of his followers—even Dan Jordan—had deserted him, LeBaron sat down to write his last and most terrible work. *The Book of the New Covenant* was a 500-page 'hit list' of about fifty people who had opposed or betrayed him and deserved to die. The text was smuggled out and some twenty copies were printed by loyalists.

On the morning of 16 August 1981, Ervil LeBaron suffered a heart attack and died. Two days later, Verlan was killed when his car hit another vehicle head on. This was one death that could not be attributed to Ervil.

THE HIT LIST

The Church of the Lamb of God fragmented after Ervil's conviction, with the largest group forming in Mexico around his eldest son, Arthur. In 1983, Arthur was shot dead during a leadership struggle, and a spate of other killings within the group followed.

It then became apparent that some of Ervil's fifty-three children had decided to act on his hit list. Dan Jordan was the first victim, shot while on a camping trip in 1987. The following year, in three separate incidents on 27 July, Mark Chynoweth, his brother Duane, Duane's eight-year-old daughter Wendy, and Eddie Marston were all shot dead.

It is estimated that as many as twenty-five people associated with LeBaron have been murdered since he died in jail. Some of his younger offspring have been tried and convicted for these murders, while others are on the run and some former followers remain in hiding. Ervil LeBaron's war may have been a small one, but there is no denying the ferocity with which it was fought.

The roof's on FIRE!

MOVE

(Founded 1973)

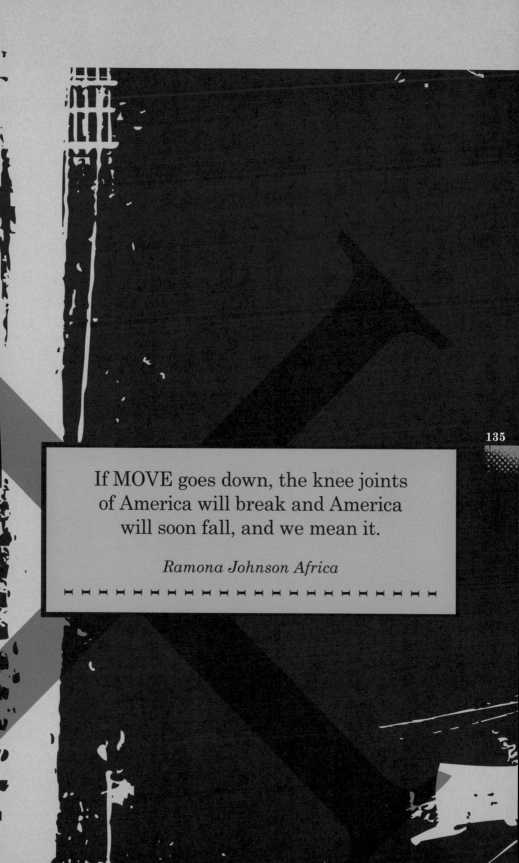

If MOVE goes down, the knee joints
of America will break and America
will soon fall, and we mean it.

Ramona Johnson Africa

ON THE HOT AND HUMID AFTERNOON OF 13 MAY 1985, the final battle between the city of Philadelphia and a tiny but vociferous religious/radical cult called MOVE had reached a stalemate. Earlier in the day, teams of heavily armed police had attempted to blast their way into MOVE's house and drive its occupants out with water cannons and tear gas. They had fired 10,000 bullets into it. Yet none of the twelve men, women and children inside had come out.

As TV cameras broadcast the operation live across America, the police hurriedly came up with a new plan. They would use a bomb to destroy the wooden bunkers MOVE had built on top of the house. Mayor Wilson Goode gave his approval, and at 5.28 p.m. a policeman in a helicopter dropped a bomb onto the roof. It exploded, starting a fire.

When told of this, Police Commissioner Gregory Sambor asked the head of the fire department if the fire could be controlled. Assured that it could, Sambor made his decision: 'Let the bunker burn.'

THE BIRTH ⊕F |⊕HN AFRICA

MOVE was born from an unlikely collaboration between a semiliterate African–American visionary and an idealistic young white social worker. The visionary was John Africa, whose real name was Vincent Lopez Leapheart. The son of Frederick and Lennie May Leapheart, he was born in Philadelphia on 26 July 1931. Educational authorities classified him as mildly retarded, and he left school at the age of sixteen. He was drafted into the army in the 1950s, and saw active service during the Korean War. Back in the United States, he is said to have earned a living as, of all things, an interior designer. He married Dorothy Clark in 1961, but they were divorced in 1967.

In 1971, Leapheart was living in Powelton Village, the gathering place for Philadelphia's hippies, dropouts and radicals, and working as an odd-job man and dog walker. He may have been a poor reader, but Leapheart was a terrific listener and mesmerizing speaker. He absorbed the ideas of the counterculture, and gained a reputation as a thinker in his own right.

One of his admirers was Donald Glassey, who had recently completed a Master's degree in social work. Leapheart moved into the cooperative housing project where Glassey lived, and the younger man began to transcribe Leapheart's philosophy, eventually producing 300 typed pages that became known as *The Book* or *The Guidelines*, and later, *The Teachings of John Africa*.

Leapheart soon ran foul of the cooperative's other tenants when his refusal to kill cockroaches in his apartment caused an infestation. He moved into a property that Glassey had bought, part of a huge Victorian mansion on North 33rd Street. Here, they started The American Christian Movement for Life, later the Christian Life Movement, eventually shortened to MOVE. Among its first two members were Leapheart's sisters, Louise James and Laverne Sims. Leapheart adopted the name John Africa, because that was the continent where life had begun. Later, all MOVE members would adopt the same surname.

John Africa preached an extreme back-to-nature philosophy, telling his followers that science and technology were 'a trick,' and they should look to animals for pointers on how to live. They were forbidden to use soap or cosmetics, and wore their hair in dreadlocks. Their diet mainly consisted of raw vegetables and fruit, but these restrictions were eased on 'distortion days,' or 'D-days,' when the adults were allowed to gorge themselves on junk food. This was justified on the grounds that 'the System' had made them addicted to such food. Their children, though, were supposed to grow up uncontaminated by it. Birdie Africa, the only child who would escape the conflagration that destroyed MOVE, recalled how they would often smell the food being cooked by adults and try to steal it. If they were caught, there would be a punishment meeting where the adults jeered and denounced them, reducing them to tears.

The women in the group were encouraged to have as many children as possible from the moment they reached childbearing age. They were to give birth naturally, forgoing medical aid, and afterward bite off the umbilical cord and eat it. Young children went naked throughout summer and wore light clothes during winter.

MOVE is not an acronym. 'It means,' according to *The Teachings of John Africa*, 'exactly what it says: MOVE, work, generate, be active. Everything that's alive moves. If it didn't, it would be stagnant, dead.' When John Africa's followers were asked what MOVE meant, they replied, 'Means MOVE.'

By the mid-1970s, MOVE had about forty members, mainly African-Americans, including a number of former alcoholics and drug addicts who credited John Africa with saving their lives. As well as taking everything that John Africa said as gospel, his followers believed that he had healing powers. The group became known within Philadelphia for their frequent, noisy demonstrations against 'the System.' They built a wooden stage at the front of their house, and delivered endless obscenity-laden diatribes over loudspeakers, driving their neighbors to distraction. Sometimes they piled into an old yellow school bus and headed off to universities, doctors' surgeries or anywhere that a politician or visiting celebrity might be making an appearance, emerging to harangue baffled passersby through megaphones. Frequently harassed and arrested by the Philadelphia police, who were not known for their lightness of touch, they were fined or spent time in jail.

The violence meted out to them by the police reached a climax—or so they claimed—with the death of a baby, Life Africa, allegedly killed during a fracas outside the MOVE house in 1976. Police denied this and said they doubted that the baby even existed (if it did, its birth had gone unregistered—although that was not unusual for a MOVE baby). MOVE summoned a group of local officials, reporters and photographers to their house one night, and showed them what they said was the decomposing body of Life Africa, which they had buried then dug up again. Whatever the truth behind this tale, the members of MOVE now began to arm themselves.

139

FIRST CONFRONTATIONS

Neighbors made constant complaints about the unsanitary conditions in the MOVE house, which was full of unvaccinated dogs and cats, cockroaches and large rats. MOVE members refused to let health inspectors into the property, and built a 8-foot high stockade fence around it. On 20 May 1977, a rumor spread that they were about to be forcibly evicted. A dozen or so MOVE members, wearing military-style clothes, paraded about on the wooden platform at the front of the house, armed with shotguns and other weapons. The house was quickly surrounded by police and members of the city's SWAT team.

Eventually, the situation was defused, but it gained MOVE much publicity. The police stepped up their surveillance of the group, and learned that Donald

Glassey had used false ID when purchasing shotguns and ammunition—a federal offence. Glassey was arrested and, facing a hefty prison sentence, turned on his comrades. He spent a day going around MOVE properties, secretly collecting much of their arsenal—shotguns, rifles, ammunition, ten completed bombs and enough materials to make about forty more. All of this was loaded into two cars and seized by police. A warrant was issued for the arrest of John Africa, who went into hiding.

Philadelphia's tough-talking mayor, Frank Rizzo, was under increasing pressure to deal with MOVE. On 16 March, a blockade of its headquarters began. Police sealed off four blocks around it, and water and electricity were cut off. MOVE's members were prepared, with plenty of food and water stockpiled. As the siege continued, they appeared on the porch every day to chat to reporters and taunt the police and the mayor. The authorities tried to negotiate with the group, offering to find them another place to live, but MOVE was in no hurry to move.

At 6 a.m. on 8 August, after hundreds of police had moved into position around the house, the Police Commissioner, Joseph O'Neill, gave the people inside two minutes to come out. When they failed to, a bulldozer moved in and demolished the stockade fence. From inside, adults and children could be heard chanting 'Baby killers! Baby killers!' and 'Long live John Africa!' After giving the occupants another chance to surrender, or at least allow the children inside to leave, police stormed the house, and the fire department began to flood the basement, where most of the MOVE members were holed up. A gunfight broke out, during which several police and fire fighters were hit, and one of them, police officer James Ramp, was killed.

Eventually, people began to emerge from the house. One MOVE member, Delbert Africa, slipped out through a side window. Though unarmed, he was set upon and beaten by police, while news cameras captured it all. (Later, three policemen were charge with assault, but acquitted.)

Eleven adults and eleven children were in the house at the time of the raid. In December 1979, nine of the adults went on trial, charged with murder, attempted murder, conspiracy and assault. Police testified that the first shots during the raid had come from the basement. Several weapons and a large amount of ammunition had been found in it after the raid, including a Ruger rifle, which a firearms expert testified had killed James Ramp. The defence produced other witnesses, including several reporters, who testified that the first shots had been fired from outside the MOVE house. The trial was characterized by disruptive behavior by the defendants, who were often ejected from proceedings.

141

The 'MOVE 9,' as they were known, had opted for trial without jury. On 8 May 1980, Judge Joseph Malmed pronounced all the defendants guilty. They were sentenced to thirty to one hundred years in prison.

While all of this had been going on, John Africa and some of his followers were living in Rochester, New York. Relations with their neighbors followed the familiar MOVE pattern, and in 1981, police raided their properties, arresting John Africa and ten others.

John Africa and one of his lieutenants, Alphonso Robbins, known as Mo Africa, went on trial, charged with bombmaking. The prosecution's chief witness was Donald Glassey, who admitted his part in making bomb threats, and claimed that John Africa had been determined to engineer a violent confrontation between MOVE and the police.

Compared to his followers, John Africa was a model of dignity and decorum in the courtroom. He emphasized his environmental credentials, saying, 'I'm fighting for air that you've got to breathe. I'm fighting for water that you've got to drink. I'm fighting for food that you've got to eat.'

On 22 July, both the defendants were found not guilty. 'The power of truth is final,' said John Africa.

THE BATTLE ⊕F ⊕SAGE AVENUE

With MOVE's Powelton headquarters bulldozed flat after the raid, the remnants of the group moved into a three-storey house owned by one of John Africa's sisters. Number 6221 Osage Avenue was part of a row of seventeen houses on a tree-lined street in West Philadelphia. A shifting group of a dozen or so people would live in this house over the next few years, including some of the children of members in prison. John Africa, who was still keeping a low profile, was often there too.

His followers were soon up to their old tricks. On Christmas Day, 1983, they started blasting their message out through loudspeakers again, demanding their imprisoned brothers and sisters be freed, and this went on most days, sometimes 24 hours a day. They threw raw meat into their yard to feed the twenty or so dogs that lived in the house. The entire block began to be infested with insects. Their neighbors petitioned the city's new African-American mayor, Wilson Goode, to do something. Goode stalled, saying he had no legal reason to evict MOVE (although there were warrants out for the arrest of two people in the house), and tried unsuccessfully to hand the problem over to federal agencies.

When MOVE announced that it was planning an action for 8 August 1984, the sixth anniversary of the Powelton shoot out, police put together a plan to raid the house. It involved using explosives to make an opening in the roof through which tear gas could be pumped. On 8 August, a hundred police and fire fighters assembled at a nearby parking lot, ready for trouble. MOVE taunted them—'We're here. We're not going anywhere'—but the day ended without confrontation.

Soon after this, MOVE stepped up the fortification of their house, building two bunkers of wood and sheet-metal on the roof. Their neighbors, some of whom had been physically attacked by MOVE members, formed an action group. The press added to calls for the mayor to do something. Coming to the conclusion that an armed confrontation with the group was now inevitable, Mayor Goode ordered Police Commissioner Gregory Sambor to prepare a new plan. The city's managing director, Leo Brooks, would be commander-in-chief of the operation.

On Saturday, 11 May, a letter written by Ramona Johnson Africa was delivered to Mayor Goode. 'If ya'll think you're gonna come in here and surprise us, you're wrong,' she wrote.

If they succeed in coming through the walls, they are going to find *smoke*, *gas*, *fire* and *bullets*. Before we let you motherfuckers make an example of us, we'll burn this motherfucking house down and burn you up with us.

On Sunday, police evacuated neighboring residents. Told that they would be able to return to their homes on Monday, most only took a change of clothes with them.

At 5.35 a.m. on Monday, Commissioner Sambor issued an ultimatum to MOVE. 'Attention, MOVE! This is America! You have to abide by the laws of the United States.'

MOVE's response came over their loudspeakers. 'We ain't got a motherfucking thing to lose, come and get us ... Is your insurance paid up? Your wives and children will cash them in after today ...'

Following the new plan, two teams under the command of officers from the Bomb Disposal Unit entered the houses on either side of 6221 Osage. They used explosives to make openings in the walls with the intention of pumping tear gas through them. They had only limited success, and were met by heavy gunfire from inside the house. The team in 6219 managed to make the largest opening, revealing a wooden bunker built inside the living room at the front of house. An officer threw a bomb at the bunker. It is believed that John Africa was killed in the explosion, which blew his head off.

Eventually both teams retreated, and by early afternoon the operation had clearly stalled. Just after 4 p.m., a party of negotiators, including the mother of one of the MOVE members, made a last effort to persuade them to come out. There was no response from the MOVE house.

The authorities had made no contingency plan for the operation lasting longer than a day, and a sense of desperation set in. The bunkers on the roof posed the biggest problem, for they meant that anyone trying to enter from the front or rear of the building could be fired on. Plans for a policeman to climb onto the roof and lodge an explosive device, or for a crane to deposit it, were briefly discussed then discarded. At 5 p.m., Managing Director Brooks rang Mayor Goode and told him they had a new plan to blow up the bunker. Brooks was later adamant that he said the bomb would be dropped from a helicopter, but Goode has always denied this. Whatever the truth of the matter, Goode was assured this latest plan would work, and approved it. Although it was known to several of the police officers involved that there were cans clearly marked 'gasoline' on the roof, no one gave the possibility of a fire much thought.

Officer Klein of the Bomb Disposal Unit was assigned to make the bomb using two sticks of Tovex TR2, a commercial explosive. Klein took it upon himself to add some C4, a powerful military explosive, to the mix. He placed the bomb in a satchel and delivered it to Lieutenant Frank Powell, who had been given the task of dropping it, and was waiting in a police helicopter.

The fire department, which had been spraying water on the house, stopped this as the helicopter appeared. Powell, wearing a harness, leaned out of the helicopter door and let the satchel drop. A minute later it exploded in a bright orange ball of flame.

Black smoke poured from the top of 6221 Osage Avenue, and the fire quickly spread to the front of the house. Just before 6 p.m. Mayor Goode, who had been watching the operation live on TV, told Leo Brooks that the fire should be extinguished, and Brooks passed this on to Sambor. It was then that Sambor had his conversation with Fire Commissioner William Richmond, and they agreed to let the fire burn until the bunker was destroyed. By 6.30 p.m., when fire fighters finally began to spray water on the flames, adjoining houses were already well alight. People who had gathered behind barricades to watch the operation grew increasingly angry, chanting 'Where's the water?' and 'Murder! Murder!'

The exact details of what happened as the fire spread down through the MOVE house will never be known.

The women and children had been in the basement since the operation began, cowering under wet blankets, and were now joined by the men. As burning debris fell into the basement, and the water that had been pumped into it began to boil, MOVE members made their way out into the alley at the back of the house, but were driven back into the smoke and flames by police gunfire. In the end only two of them, Ramona Africa and thirteen-year-old Birdie Africa, made it out alive.

RECRIMINATI⊕NS

Philadelphians awoke the next day to an apocalyptic scene. The fire had raged through the block and the surrounding area, destroying sixty-one homes and leaving about 260 people homeless. Eleven MOVE members were dead—six adults and five children.

Mayor Goode quickly announced there would be an independent inquiry into the tragedy. The 'MOVE Commission' sat for eight months, interviewed hundreds of people and pored over thousands of documents. Its report was scathing about the poor planning of the operation, the failure to evacuate the children before it began, the lack of communication among commanders, and the excessive use of automatic weapons and explosives. It concluded that the deaths of the children 'appear to be unjustified homicides which should be investigated by a grand jury.' Ramona Africa, who had been jailed after the fire, and the families of the five dead children filed suits against some of the officials involved (Mayor Goode had been granted immunity). These were eventually settled out of court, and the city also agreed to pay Birdie Africa $1.7 million. In 1996, a jury found that the city of Philadelphia, Sambor and Richmond were guilty of using excessive force and violating the

MOVE members' constitutional rights, and Ramona and the relatives of two of the adult victims were awarded $1.5 million in compensation.

In the years following the conflagration in Osage Avenue, Ramona Africa and a few others continued to campaign for the release of the MOVE 9, who became eligible for parole in 2008. And the teachings of arch-technophobe John Africa live on through the internet.

Off on a Comet

Heaven's Gate

(Founded 1975)

Our 22 years of classroom here on planet Earth is finally coming to conclusion—'graduation' from the human evolutionary level. We are happily prepared to leave this world with Ti's crew.

Marshall Herff Applewhite

ON THE AFTERNOON OF **26 MARCH 1997,** two sheriff's deputies arrived at a sprawling mansion in Rancho Santa Fe, a wealthy enclave of San Diego, California. They were responding to an anonymous report that the house was the scene of a mass suicide. Opening the front door, they were hit with an overpowering stench that left little doubt that the report was true.

Thirty-nine bodies were found in the house. Most were lying on their backs, hands by their sides, on metallic bunk beds. All were dressed identically in long-sleeved black shirts, black pants and brand new black and white Nike shoes. Purple sheets, neatly folded into diamond shapes, were draped over the bodies. Many had a five-dollar bill and loose change in their pants pockets, while next to them were travel bags packed with a change of clothes. All the bodies had shaven heads, leading to an initial report that they were all males. (In fact, nineteen were male, twenty female.) On each black shirt was sewn a triangular patch reading 'Heaven's Gate Away Team.'

Investigators, finding their first clues on the computers in the house, began to piece together the story. All of the deceased were members of a self-proclaimed 'UFO cult' called Heaven's Gate, led by sixty-five-year-old Marshall Applewhite, who was found among the dead. Applewhite and his partner Bonnie Lu Nettles (who died in 1985) had founded the group more than twenty years earlier. They believed themselves to be extraterrestrial beings who had come from 'The Evolutionary Level Above Heaven,' and offered their followers the promise that they, too, could attain this level. The trigger for the mass suicide had been the appearance of the exceptionally bright Comet Hale-Bopp, which had been visible in the night skies since early 1996, and which, according to a rumor, was being trailed by a UFO. Applewhite had taken this to be the signal that he and his followers had long been waiting for—the go-ahead to shed the inferior 'vehicles' of their bodies and travel to the next level, in outer space.

THE MUSIC TEACHER

Marshall Herff Applewhite was born in Spur, Texas, in 1932. After graduating from college in 1952 he married Ann Pierce. The son of a Presbyterian minister, Applewhite considered becoming one too, and spent a year at a seminary, but changed his mind and embarked on a career in music. A talented singer and musician, he was the choirmaster at a church in North Carolina for a couple of years, and sang the lead roles in productions of South Pacific and Oklahoma at the University of Colorado.

In 1961, Applewhite, who now had two children, became a music teacher at the University of Alabama. A handsome man with striking blue eyes, he charmed and inspired those around him. He suffered a setback, however, when he was suspended from this position, apparently after being discovered having a sexual relationship with a male student. He left Alabama—and his wife and children— and moved to Houston, Texas, where he lived openly as a homosexual. In 1966, he was appointed an assistant professor at a private Catholic college in Houston, and in his spare time sang with the city's Grand Opera. He had been highly regarded as a music teacher wherever he worked, but in 1970 he lost his job at the college. It seems this was the result of internal politics, but there were also rumors of another liaison with a student.

Applewhite was hospitalized in 1972. His family later said this was because of a heart condition, while others claimed he was suffering from a drug-induced mental breakdown. (One suggestion is that he had checked himself in to be 'cured' of his homosexuality.) Whatever the reason for his being there, it was in the hospital that the momentous meeting took place between Marshall Applewhite and Bonnie Lu Trusdale Nettles.

Nettles was born in Houston in 1911. She trained to be a nurse, married and had four children. She was fascinated by the occult, astrology, theosophy and tarot cards, claimed to have psychic abilities, and said that she was aided in her readings by the spirit of a Franciscan monk, 'Brother Francis,' who died in 1818.

Applewhite and Nettles made an odd couple. He was tall and handsome, she plain and dumpy. They formed an immediate bond, however. They were convinced they had known each other in previous lives, and came to believe that they had been put on Earth for a special purpose. As ill matched as they seemed, each had something the other needed. Applewhite was, by all accounts, ashamed of his homosexuality. He longed to have a deep but asexual relationship, and Nettles fitted the bill (they would never have sexual relations). Meanwhile, the charismatic Applewhite, who had developed an interest in the occult, seemed to Nettles the means by which she could satisfy her spiritual ambitions. She deserted her family for him.

B⊕ AND PEEP

Having decided that they had a common destiny, Applewhite and Nettles had to find out what it might be. They embarked on an intensive study of Christianity and alternative religions. For a while, they ran the Christian Arts Center, located in a Unitarian Universalist church in Houston, which hosted talks on astrology, mysticism and other New Age beliefs. At one point, Applewhite suffered another breakdown or, as he put it, 'near-death experience,' during which he believed that God had spoken to him. He and Nettles began to put more faith in dreams, visions and the voices they heard in their heads than anything they read in books.

The Christian Arts Center closed after about a year. Applewhite and Nettles traveled aimlessly around the country in a convertible sports car, doing odd jobs or relying on the charity of churches to survive. When their car broke down in Oregon in 1974, they were forced to camp there for two months. It was here that the final revelation of their destiny came to them.

The philosophy that Applewhite and Nettles came up with combined elements of Christianity, theosophy (especially its belief in superhuman beings called the 'Ascended Masters') and science fiction. They believed that Heaven, or the Kingdom of God, was a physical place in which dwelt beings who had reached 'The Evolutionary Level Above Human.' These beings, who physically resembled the bald, bulbous-headed aliens found in much UFO lore, were androgynous, communicated telepathically and were free of all human and animal instincts, including sexuality. Applewhite and Nettles believed that 'Representatives' from Heaven sometimes traveled to Earth, where they sought out promising individuals who could move to the next level. Jesus Christ had been one such 'Representative,' and Applewhite and Nettles were his successors. They started to call themselves 'The Two,' after the two prophets mentioned in the Book of Revelation who are killed by a 'beast' but rise from the dead three days later and are taken to heaven on 'a cloud.' All of this, said Applewhite and Nettles, would happen to them, and quite soon. The cloud, though, would be a spaceship. As for the other inhabitants of Earth, some of them lacked souls, while the bodies of others were occupied by evil aliens called Luciferians—obviously the equivalent of the Bible's fallen angels.

The Two's first follower was a woman named Sharon Walsh. She left her husband to join them, but made the mistake of taking the family car with her. Her husband reported it stolen, and Applewhite and Nettles were arrested in Texas and charged with a variety of offences, including credit card abuse. Applewhite spent six months in jail. Following his release, he and Nettles traveled to California, where they held numerous meetings, often on university campuses. Posters and flyers advertising these events played up the UFO connection. 'UFOs ...' read a typical one. 'Why they are here? Who have they come for? When will they leave?' People who turned up to the meetings were told that the group were not seeking converts, only supplying information. They learned that The Two, while still looking outwardly human, had almost completed their physical metamorphosis, and within months there would be a 'demonstration' (their death and resurrection) that would prove their claims.

These meetings were a great success, and dozens of people joined. The group was now calling itself HIM (Human Individual Metamorphosis), while Applewhite and Nettles had taken on the childish names 'Bo' and 'Peep,' a reference to their status as 'shepherds.'

Bo and Peep, with shifting numbers of followers in tow, continued their wanderings. In September 1975, they held a meeting at the Bayshore Inn in Waldpost, Oregon. They were clearly very persuasive that night, for some twenty-three people who attended it decided to immediately give up their possessions and families to join Bo and Peep. Their 'disappearance' caused headlines across the country, with some of the initial reports suggesting that they had actually been taken away in a UFO. The media would continue to take a keen interest in the group over the next few years.

Bo and Peep had up to 200 followers by now, although many did not stay for long. Some found it difficult to live by their rules—which included cutting off all relations with family members and abstaining from sex—especially when the promised 'demonstration' failed to take place. Then, in April 1976, Bo and Peep took the unusual step of announcing they would not be accepting anymore members. They gathered their existing members at a camping ground in Wyoming for a 'classroom,' intending to weed out those who weren't worthy of the 'next level'. When this wound up, seventy followers remained. This core group continued to live in camp grounds until one of the followers inherited $300,000, which allowed them to rent two houses in Colorado and Texas. By now, Applewhite and Nettles had changed their names again, and were calling themselves Do and Ti (after musical notes). Reports of the group's activities continued to appear in magazines and newspapers, and they even inspired a TV pilot called *The Mysterious Two*, which aired on NBC in 1982. It told the story of two evangelists who turned out to be aliens on a recruiting drive. The Applewhite character was played by John Forsythe of *Dynasty* fame.

FLIGHT TRAINING

Do and Ti demanded that their followers make a complete break with their pasts, give up all material possessions and donate any money they had to the group. They were also given new names, generally based on a formula of three letters (usually of some symbolic significance) followed by the suffix 'ody.' This resulted in such bizarre combinations as Srrody, Qstody and Stmody.

The group's members lived according to a set of rules designed to prepare them for both life at the next level and the voyage in the spaceship that would transport them to it. Each day ran to a rigid schedule that specified their activities to the minute. Men and women had their hair cut short and wore identical clothes, usually jumpsuits that concealed the shape of the body. (At one point, they spent three months wearing hoods with mirrored eye slits.) They were encouraged to talk as little as possible, in preparation for the time when they would communicate telepathically. Applewhite handled all the finances, and while members could leave the group's houses, they were only allowed to carry a five-dollar bill, and some loose change in case they needed to make a phone call. (This accounted for the money found on the bodies after the mass suicide.) Alcohol, tobacco and drugs were forbidden.

The most important ban was the one on sexual relations. Sex was, for Applewhite, the ultimate manifestation of the human and animal instincts he was trying to transcend. In the videotape he made to be broadcast after the suicides, he said, 'we are all totally celibate and there is no relationship in the nature of the male or female, there is no sexuality, there is no sensuality, that is very distasteful to us.' At some point, Applewhite had decided to have himself castrated. Seven other male members followed his example.

After the flurry of publicity in the late '70s, the group closed in on itself and little was heard from them during the '80s. In 1982, Nettles wrote to her daughter, Terrie, telling her that she had cancer and one of her eyes had been removed. According to Terrie, she wrote again in 1984, saying that she wanted to leave the group but 'there wasn't a graceful way to leave.' She died the following year. Applewhite was devastated, but said that he maintained contact with Ti telepathically. After that, an empty chair was provided for Ti at all the group's meetings.

THE AWAY TEAⅢ

In May 1993, the group reemerged with a full-page ad in *USA Today* and other newspapers, headed 'UFO Cult Resurfaces with Final Offer.' Their writings had now taken on a markedly apocalyptic tone. Civilization was about to be recycled or, to use Do's favorite phrase, 'spaded over.' They had changed their name again, and were now called Total Overcomers Anonymous.

At this point some of the original members from the 1970s who had left years earlier returned to the group—usually after suffering setbacks in their lives—and a few new members joined. Some of them set up a webpage design company called Higher Source, which was quite successful. In June 1995, some of the money it had brought in was used to buy 40 acres of land in Manzano, New Mexico. The group's members set up tents to live in, and began to build an 'earth ship,' a structure made of recycled tires and dirt, which, in theory, would need no artificial heating or cooling. There were grand plans for the settlement, which was to include a bakery and pharmacy. In April 1996, however, with the 'earth ship' still not completed, Do changed his mind. The property was sold and the group rented the seven-bedroom mansion at 18241 Colina Norte, Rancho Santa Fe, its last address.

The mansion was sparsely furnished, with little more than bunk beds and dozens of computers. There were shelves filled with science fiction books and, in the living room, a 72-inch TV screen on which they watched their favorite shows, including *Star Trek* and *The X-Files*. While the lifestyle of the group was austere, there were occasional treats. Every fortnight, three members went into town and returned with strawberry pancakes for everybody.

The group, which had now taken on the name Heaven's Gate, was a mixed lot, with ages ranging from twenty-six

157

to seventy-two. In a curious twist, among their number was Thomas Nichols, the brother of Nichelle Nichols, who played Lieutenant Uhura in *Star Trek*. Like some of the other members, Nichols had not been in contact with his family for decades.

There is no doubt that the group's decision to finally leave this world was influenced by Do's deteriorating health—his 'container,' as he referred to his body, was failing. It seems that he told some people he was suffering from terminal cancer (although no trace of this was found at his autopsy). It is equally certain that the timing of their exit was determined by the appearance of Comet Hale-Bopp. In November 1996, an amateur astronomer took a photograph of it that showed, he claimed, a UFO in its tail. Scientists quickly dismissed the object as a star, but the story captured the imagination of UFO enthusiasts across the world. A 'red alert' was placed on the group's website—'Hale-Bopp brings closure to Heaven's Gate.'

In their last days, Do and his followers decided to enjoy themselves a little, going on a four-day bus trip at the beginning of March 1997. On 19 March, after recording their farewell video messages, they went to see the Mike Leigh movie *Secrets and Lies*, and had pizza for dinner. On 21 March, they had a final lunch at a nearby restaurant, ordering thirty-nine identical meals of chicken pot pie, cheesecake and iced tea.

The suicides were planned and carried out with typical orderliness. Each member consumed Phenobarbitol mixed with either applesauce or pudding, washed it down with vodka, then placed a plastic bag over their head and fastened it with a rubber band. The deaths took place in three stages over several days, with the first group probably dying on 22 March. After their bodies were cleaned and laid out by the other members, a further group took the lethal mixture, leaving three female members to make the final arrangements before they, too, embarked on their journey to the next level.

As the story of the mass suicide broke, the world's media pored over the material that Applewhite and his followers had left behind, including the rambling writings on their website, and videos in which the members, all shaven-headed like their leader, said goodbye to their families and explained the reasons for their actions. 'We couldn't be happier about what we're about to do,' said one woman. 'This will bring me just the happiest day of my life,' said a man. Most of the coverage inevitably portrayed Applewhite as a maniac who had fooled his followers into taking their lives with the spurious promise of a trip into space. But the idea is difficult to sustain. Since the group's beginnings, The Two had argued that only the most dedicated and worthy would make it through to the next level, and often seemed to actively discourage potential followers.

159

The philosophy of Heaven's Gate, for all its science fiction trappings, embodied ideas that have circulated around Christianity for aeons. That the physical world is inherently evil can be found in a host of heretical groups, usually described as 'gnostic.' There is little doubt that the members of Heaven's Gate believed these ideas, and were attracted to them because of disappointments in their own lives. About a quarter of those who died in 1997 had joined in the 1970s and, for all the rigid restrictions imposed on them, the group seems to have been genuinely happy living together. On the evidence of the farewell videos, they were also happy to die together. They did not, however, believe they were committing suicide.

Moses, Murder and ⁀U⊹I⌐A⊹I⊕N

The Ant Hill Kids
(Founded 1977)

I have inflicted on myself mental wounds whose invisible scars I will carry for the rest of my life. Some of these scars will remain particularly vivid, such as the ones created when I carried out the folly of my fury: traumatizing, mutilating and inflicting suffering on the members of my entourage ...

Roch Thériault

Outside of his drinking bouts, he is a very good man.

Nicole Ruel

WHEN HE WAS SOBER, ROCH THÉRIAULT WAS A CHARMER. He sang songs, told jokes and could talk about any subject that came up. With a few bottles of beer or cognac under his belt, however, the heavily-bearded, self-styled reincarnation of Moses was an altogether different proposition. There is often an element of sadism in the behavior of cult leaders—and a corresponding element of masochism in their followers—but rarely have sadism and masochism reached such extremes as in the extraordinary, almost unbelievable saga of Thériault and his eight wives.

THE WOODWORKER

Roch (sometimes spelled Rock) Thériault was born on 16 May 1947, in a small village in what is now the city of Sanguenay in Quebec, Canada. His parents, Hyacinthe and Pierrette Thériault, were devout Catholics, and Roch was one of eight children. When he was six, the family moved to Thetford Mines, a town built upon the world's largest deposit of asbestos.

Hyacinthe was a member of the White Berets, an ultra-conservative Catholic society. He liked to take his kids with him, little white berets on their heads, when he went out seeking donations. This didn't endear them to the locals, and instilled in Roch a bitter hatred of Catholicism.

Roch told two main stories about his childhood. The first was that his father was a drunk who savagely beat him. The second was that he spent much of his time roaming forests close to his home, communing with nature and playing with bears. There seems to be little or no truth in either of these tales. In fact, Thériault's childhood was uneventful. Alone among his family, he liked reading books, and he was a good student, although he dropped out of school early.

In 1967 he married Francine Grenier. A skilled woodworker, he built a house of rough-hewn pine, and they had two children, Roch, Jr. and Françoise. In 1970, Thériault had an operation for duodenal ulcers in which a large part of his stomach was removed. This left him in severe pain and unable to digest food properly, and led to significant personality changes. He became self-pitying and obsessed with his own health, studied medical textbooks and told people he had cancer. He started to drink heavily. He also became obsessed with sex, pursuing other women and, at one point, asking Francine's parents whether they would mind him setting up a nudist colony on their land. The marriage did not survive.

Most who knew Thériault well traced the beginnings of his descent into madness to his stomach operation. It seems that a great deal of mayhem could have been avoided had it been known then, as it is now, that ulcers are usually caused by an infection and can be treated with antibiotics.

For all his problems, Thériault remained a gregarious and popular individual. He began a relationship with a girl from Quebec City, Gisèle Tremblay, and supported himself with his woodworking skills (his wooden beer mugs were quite a hit). He became interested in the occult and joined a Catholic-affiliated secret society, the Aramis Club. He was appointed president of its initiation committee, and startled the other members by suggesting that they wear capes imprinted with an image of Satan.

Then he switched allegiances and joined the Seventh Day Adventists. He excelled at attracting converts, and was put in charge of their five-day stop-smoking clinics. In 1977, four young Adventists, Jacques Fiset, Solange Boilard, Francine Laflamme and Chantal Labrie, came under his spell. He encouraged them to visit Thetford

163

Mines on weekends, and stay at his girlfriend Gisèle's one-bedroom apartment, where he would preach to them for hours on end. Another girl, Nicole Ruel, moved in permanently. Gisèle, who was subjected to constant lectures by Thériault on women's God-ordained subservience to men, had little say in all this. Still hoping to marry Thériault, she was particularly put out by the arrival of the attractive and outspoken Gabrielle Lavalée. A trained nurse, Gabrielle had grown disillusioned with Western medicine, and was interested in the holistic methods that Thériault advocated. Two other girls, Marise Lambert and Josée Pelletier, also joined at this point, along with a twenty-four-year-old former drug addict named Claude Ouellette.

Thériault and his band traveled around Canada, holding stop-smoking clinics that ended with a vegetarian banquet. He attracted more followers, including the ineffectual Jacques Giguére and his more spirited wife, Maryse Grenier (no relation to Francine). The group was now too large to fit into Gisèle's tiny apartment, and Thériault rented a house in Sainte Marie, south of Quebec City. This became The Healthy Living Clinic, which sold Adventist literature and health foods. Thériault obtained supplies from an Adventist wholesaler, and sold them at heavily marked-up prices.

In May 1978, Thériault persuaded a thirty-eight-year-old woman named Geraldine Auclair, then undergoing hospital treatment for leukemia, that he could cure her with natural methods. She died at the clinic a few weeks later. The police found there was nothing they could charge Thériault with, but the Adventists decided they had now had enough of their overzealous member with the unusual living arrangements. He was promptly expelled from the church.

INTⓄ THE WILDERNESS

Thériault wasn't too bothered about the expulsion, although having his supply of cheap Adventist goods cut off meant the clinic would no longer be financially viable. Abandoning it, he and his group, which now consisted of twelve women, six men and two children, hit the road. They ended up in the Gaspé peninsula, a remote area on the south shore of the Saint Lawrence River. It was here that Thériault had a revelation about the end of the world, which would involve earthquakes and enormous hailstones falling from the sky, and take place on 17 February 1979. Their only hope was to remain in the wilderness, where they would await Christ's return.

Thériault's followers built an octagonal log cabin, working tirelessly to get it completed before winter set in. Only allowed meagre rations by their leader, they were constantly hungry. Meanwhile, Thériault had abandoned vegetarianism and gorged himself on junk food.

Some tired of the hardships and left. Those who remained were given biblical names by Thériault, with his own being 'Moses.' As befitting an Old Testament-style prophet, he announced that he was entitled to multiple wives. He had married Gisèle while still running the Healthy Living Clinic; he now took as 'concubines' Nicole, Josée, Marise, Francine, Gabrielle, Chantal and Solange. All would eventually have at least one of his children.

He was also drinking again, and when drunk would fly into violent rages. Jacques Giguére's wife, Maryse, was often a target. Once, when she had eaten two pancakes without his permission, he punched her, breaking two ribs. On another occasion, when she talked about leaving, he ordered Jacques to cut off one of her toes with an ax. When Jacques baulked at this, Thériault shouted,

'Don't you have any balls? If you want to be a man, you have to learn how to teach your woman a lesson.' Jacques did as he was told.

The end of the world date, 17 February, came and went. 'Moses' explained that he had miscalculated.

THE DEATH ⊕F SAⅢUEL

In November 1988, a mentally deficient twenty-three-year-old man named Guy Veer left the hospital in Quebec City where he was being treated for depression, and made his way to Thériault's commune. He was allowed to stay, but was kept apart from the main group and made to sleep in a shed. Veer was put in charge of the three children in the commune who had not been fathered by Thériault, including Jacques and Maryse's two-year-old son, Samuel.

In March 1989, Thériault threw a party to celebrate the arrival of his two sons from his first marriage. Veer, as usual, was not invited. Although the details of what followed are hazy, it seems that during the night, unable to stop Samuel crying, Veer punched him several times. The bruises this left were apparent the next day, and Thériault assigned Gabrielle to look after him. That night, Thériault suddenly decided that the baby needed to be circumcised. After squirting ethanol into Samuel's mouth as an anesthetic, he performed the operation with a razor blade. The next day, Samuel was found dead.

Thériault blamed Veer for the death. Months later, he ordered that Veer stand trial, and assigned the roles of judge, prosecutor, jury and so on to various group members. Veer was found not guilty by reason of insanity, but Thériault then called for a vote on whether he should be castrated. The motion was carried. Veer protested, but Thériault talked him into it, telling him that the headaches he had been suffering lately were caused by a diseased testicle. Veer even signed a piece of paper, giving his consent.

Veer was made to lie on a table. With Gabrielle the nurse assisting, and Claude and Jacques holding down his legs, Thériault sliced open his scrotum and removed his testicles.

Thériault continued to torture him after that, on one occasion tying him to a tree and whipping him. Fearing for his life, Veer finally escaped. He told people about the death of Samuel, and the commune was raided by police, who arrested Thériault, Jacques and Maryse. They also took away the seven remaining children on the property, including twelve-year-old Roch, Jr., who had been made to take part in the castration.

Seven commune members were charged with offences relating to Samuel's death, while Thériault and Gabrielle were also charged with causing bodily harm to Guy Veer. Thériault was jailed for two years, Gabrielle for nine months, and Claude and Jacques for six months. Police burned the settlement at the Gaspé. The children were returned to their mothers, on the condition that they no longer lived as a group.

While in prison, Thériault kept in contact with his followers by telephone. He also used the time to write a syrupy autobiography, which played up the communion with nature, and played down the death and castration.

BURNT RIVER

On his release from prison, Thériault decided it was time to get out of Quebec. After scouting around Ontario, he purchased a 200-acre property near the tiny township of Burnt River in Victoria County. The group now consisted of Thériault, his eight wives,

Claude, Jacques and Maryse, and ten children. They began to build another settlement, but ran into financial problems. In Quebec, Thériault had arranged for the welfare payments of all his followers to be paid into his bank account. In Ontario, however, social services classified them as an institution rather than a family, and denied them welfare. Thériault sent his people out shoplifting, but after some of them were caught, they were banned from shopping in the nearby town of Lindsay.

After raising some cash by selling fruit, they were able to buy the equipment for a bakery. They formed a company that Thériault named The Ant Hill Kids— because they all worked together like ants.

With the second version of his community established, Thériault grew bored and began to drink heavily again, using his stomach pains as an excuse. His binges would last up to three days, and the violence meted out to his hapless followers during them was severe. Angered by their behavior, or just on a whim, he struck them with hammers or axes. He made them strip naked and stand outside in the cold for hours, or lie on the ground while he urinated on them. He pulled out eleven of Claude's teeth with pliers, and burned Josée's back and shoulders with an acetylene torch. He systematically cut, punched, stabbed and shot at all of them, or made them fight each other. Only once did one of them strike back, when Jacques punched him in the face. Jacques' punishment was to be circumcised then and there.

When he sobered up again, Thériault felt terrible about what God had made him do to his followers, and was solicitous in tending their wounds. They didn't blame him, having been convinced that their salvation depended on suffering in this life. Sometimes after a particularly brutal piece of ill-treatment, they wrote him letters thanking him.

Meanwhile, the local Children's Aid Society had begun to take a keen interest in Thériault's group. They had learned of his activities in Quebec, and its officers visited the commune regularly. As the women refused to talk, and the children showed no obvious signs of physical abuse, they were powerless to take any action.

The breakthrough came when Maryse left the group. She had long begged Thériault to let her go, and he finally relented. He allowed her to take her two youngest children, but made her leave the eldest, Miriam. In an effort to get Miriam out as well, Maryse went to the authorities and told them horrifying tales of the children's treatment. They were, she said, divided into two groups. Those that Thériault had fathered were the chosen ones; those he had not were considered slaves, made to do menial tasks and systematically starved. In his drunken rages, Thériault threw children against trees and walls. He also engaged in sexual activities with them, including masturbating in front of them.

On 6 December 1986, police and child aid workers raided the commune and removed thirteen children, who were placed with foster parents. Many showed signs of being extremely disturbed, and further lurid details of sexual abuse came out during interviews. In October 1987, a judge ordered that they be made permanent wards of the state, along with four more children who had been born since the raid. The exception was Miriam, who was returned to Maryse. Once this happened, she refused to say anything more to the police. They decided that there was insufficient evidence to prosecute Thériault and the other adults on child abuse charges.

169

THE AMATEUR SURGEⴲN

Despite being one of his first converts, Solange Boilard had initially been a little more sceptical about Thériault's prophetic status than the others, and had been the last to become a concubine. Since then, she had become one of his most ardent followers. She was his second-in-command, ran the Ant Hill Kids business, and seems to have been the wife he loved the most.

One night in September 1988, Thériault was drunk again. Solange had been suffering from stomach pains, and Thériault, the medical expert, had diagnosed kidney problems. He decided that he needed to operate.

Solange lay on the table in the bakery. Thériault administered an enema of molasses and water. Turning her over, he punched her a couple of times in the stomach, then picked up a knife. He made an incision about five inches long below her rib cage, pulled out part of her intestine and broke it off with his fingers. She was sewn up and Thériault ordered her to walk around. She never said a word during all of this. She was allowed to stagger off to bed.

Francine and Gabrielle watched over her that night. One of the last things she said was, 'Well, I never thought I would suffer that much in my life.' She died in agony the next day.

It seems that Thériault really believed in his powers as a healer, and was as shocked as anyone by Solange's death. He even grieved for her, but being Roch Thériault, his grief manifested itself in unusual ways. Solange was buried in a pine coffin, but he had her exhumed repeatedly over the next couple of weeks. He ordered that her kidneys and uterus be removed. He had her skull opened up so he could masturbate into it, apparently in an attempt to bring her back to life. He removed part of a rib, which he made into a necklace. Other bones were distributed among the commune members as keepsakes. Thériault told them that he believed Solange had entered his body, and he was going to give birth to her. They eventually persuaded him to let them cremate what was left of her body.

Thériault blamed his followers for Solange's death. They were often forced to flee into the bush and hide there until his drunken rages had subsided. Gabrielle Lavalée, always the most strong-willed of the wives, now bore the brunt of his attacks.

One night, about a month after Solange's death, Gabrielle complained of a toothache. Thériault seized a pair of pliers and yanked out eight of her teeth, taking part of her jawbone as well. He then went after her with a knife. As she attempted to fend him off, he cut two of the tendons in her right hand.

Gabrielle escaped to a women's shelter, where she was treated by a dentist and a doctor, who put wires in her hand. Thériault tracked her down to the shelter, and persuaded her to return.

On the evening of 26 July 1989, Thériault was in a good mood, drinking and boasting of his surgical skills— which was enough to cause Gisèle and some of the others to flee. He asked to examine Gabrielle's injured hand. When she placed it on the kitchen table, he drove a hunting knife through it. She wasn't able to extract the knife and stood there with her hand impaled, her arm turning purple.

After almost an hour, Thériault pulled the knife out, then picked up a smaller carpet knife. He began gouging flesh out of Gabrielle's arm between her shoulder and elbow but, too drunk to go on, made Chantal finish the job. With the bone completely exposed, he severed the arm with a meat cleaver.

The next day, he stitched up the stump. Gabrielle faced further tortures in the name of treatment over the next three weeks. It wasn't until Thériault, deciding that her arm wasn't healing properly, cauterized it with a red-hot chunk of metal (badly burning the rest of her body in the process) that she mustered the determination to escape for good. She checked herself into a hospital, saying that she had been in a car accident and her boyfriend had been forced to amputate her arm.

The police didn't believe her. Arriving at the commune, they found it deserted. Thériault, Jacques, Chantal and Nicole went into hiding (along with two babies whose births they had managed to conceal from the authorities). They were arrested six weeks later. Thériault surprised everyone by pleading guilty to charges relating to Gabriele's amputation—he clearly believed that by doing so he would be able to keep the death of Solange a secret. He didn't know that on the day of his arrest, Gisèle had finally told the police about her terrible end.

UP F⊕R PAR⊕LE

Thériault was charged with second-degree murder. The police compiled a dossier of eighty-four serious attacks that he had inflicted on his followers during their time in Ontario. When Thériault's legal team became aware of this, he agreed to plead guilty to the murder charge, on condition that he face no further charges. Before sentencing, he made a florid speech in which he accepted that he should be put behind bars. 'I made myself an odious character,' he said, 'an incontestable master compelled undetectably by my own will.' He was sentenced to life imprisonment.

Three of his wives, Chantal, Nicole and Francine, remain faithful to him, and thanks to conjugal visits, he has even been able to father more children while in prison (taking the total to more than thirty). He is said to be a model prisoner, and became eligible for parole in 1999. Gabrielle Lavalée, who wrote a book about her years with Thériault, was present when parole was denied in 2002. 'The population, myself included, will be able to have a long night's sleep tonight,' she said.

Son of a
BLACK G⊕D

Nation of Yahweh
(Founded 1979)

I'm the supreme narcissist. I'm the one who gets off on myself supremely. I look in the mirror and say, 'You're lookin' good ... the best lookin' man in the universe.'

Yahweh Ben Yahweh

MIAMI, FLORIDA, HAS NEVER HAD A SHORTAGE OF MURDERS, but during the first half of 1986, bodies began turning up on its streets with even greater frequency than usual. It didn't take long for the police to notice a curious pattern in some of these killings. The victims were all white males, they had been stabbed and mutilated, and most of them were found missing an ear. The police suspected a serial killer was at work.

In fact, what they were seeing were the first casualties in a racial war. It was a war with an unlikely instigator—a charismatic black religious leader, respected by many in the community for his good works. He went by many names—Brother Love, Moses Israel, Yashua the Messiah. It was perhaps the last name he adopted, Yahweh Ben Yahweh, that gives the greatest insight into the image he had of himself. It means God, the Son of God.

G⊕D'S GIFT T⊕ THE W⊕RLD

Hulon Mitchell, Jr. knew he was divinely gifted. He was born on 27 October 1935 in Kingfisher, Oklahoma, the first child of a Pentecostal minister, the Reverend Hulon Mitchell, and his wife, Pearl, who would go on to have fourteen other children. From the age of three, Hulon, Jr. was playing an enthusiastic part in his father's church services. Later, along with his siblings, he sang with the family's traveling gospel show, the Musical Mitchells. He married in 1954 and had four children, but the marriage didn't last. After a stint in the air force, he studied psychology at university, and got involved in the civil rights movement.

In 1964, Mitchell and his second wife, Chloe, moved to Atlanta, Georgia, where he joined the quasi-Muslim, segregationist Nation of Islam (NOI). Renouncing his 'slave name,' he became Hulon X, then was given the spiritual name Shah. He became one of the NOI's most effective ministers, but his career was short-lived. Allegations of sexual improprieties reached the NOI's headquarters, and its leader, Elijah Muhammed, ordered an investigation. Minister Shah quietly resigned.

The mercurial Mitchell reinvented himself as a radio evangelist named Father Michel. He and his partner Billy Jones (Father Jone) became known in Atlanta as 'the prophets' because of their claimed abilities to see into the future and predict winning lottery numbers. Their church suffered a setback when three men burst into Father Jone's apartment and shot him dead, but Father Michel carried on, his miraculous powers growing by the day. He could cure all bodily ills and make people rich by prayer. He wore a long white robe and a golden crown, and asked his followers to call him 'the King.'

Father Michel had big plans for his church and donations rolled in, but it soon collapsed. Disgruntled ex-members later attempted to sue Father Michel for fraud, but by then he had left both Atlanta and his wife behind.

He bounced back in 1976 as Brother Love, preaching on the streets of Orlando, Florida. His followers included a group of women who supported him financially and, it was said, in other ways. One of them, a mother of three named Linda Gaines, became his closest companion. He was also busy studying religious texts and developing yet another spiritual persona.

Mitchell had become disillusioned with the civil rights movement and believed, as the Nation of Islam did, that segregation was the way forward for black people. He denounced traditional black preachers—who of course included his father—as 'dirty dogs' who lay down in front of whites and betrayed their own people.

The Nation of Islam also taught him that the original humans were blacks, and whites their genetically inferior descendents. They pointed to a verse in Genesis where it is said that the seed of Abraham 'shall be a stranger in a land that is not theirs, and shall serve them; and they shall afflict them four hundred years,' and interpreted this to mean the near-400 years of slavery that blacks had endured in America. Mitchell, while retaining these ideas, turned from Islam to Judaism, and learned that the Jews considered 'Yahweh' to be the one true name of God. Intensive study of the Bible proved to him that the Jews and Jesus had been black, as indeed was Yahweh. It was, he said, 'the world's best-kept secret.'

There was nothing new in these ideas. Since the late nineteenth century, a number of so-called 'Black Hebrew Israelite' sects had taught that the biblical Jews were black. What was new was the apocalyptic urgency that Mitchell brought to his theme. The final violent battle between blacks and whites was coming, and after that, the Promised Land. It would prove an electrifying message to some.

THE TEMPLE OF LOVE

Mitchell returned to his family in Oklahoma long enough to convert a few of them to his new beliefs, including his sister Jean. In 1980, Jean and about twenty others moved to Miami to be with Ok Moshe Israel, as Mitchell was now known, or Moses for short. Linda Gaines, now called Sister Judith, was his second-in-command.

His disciples walked the streets of Miami, handing out fliers and spreading the word. The men grew long beards and the women stopped straightening their hair. They adopted new names—Israel for their surname and a first name picked from the Bible. Moses encouraged them to donate 10 percent of their income to the cause, and bought a derelict warehouse occupying a whole city block. One hundred and fifty followers worked hard to make the building habitable, and Moses persuaded thirty of them to live there permanently. It was renamed the Temple of Love.

Inside, the Temple came to resemble a miniature town with its own cafeteria, grocery store and ice-cream parlor. There was a school where the children learned rudimentary Hebrew, and a print shop that turned out copies of Moses' books. The inhabitants lived in cubicles separated by partitions, and followed a strict regime of work and prayer. To keep the outside world out, Moses appointed a security force, the Circle of Ten. Its members patrolled the property armed with wooden staffs.

A number of followers soon became disillusioned with their new messiah. His sermons were full of racial hatred and he seemed oddly preoccupied with sex. He insisted that sex should only be for procreation, yet could often be seen slipping into cubicles where young girls were sleeping. (Later, Sister Judith's daughter, Sara, would allege that he began having sex with her when she was ten years old.) There were reports of strange goings-on at midwifery classes where Moses was the only male present. He also personally inspected male followers to make sure they were circumcised, and at one point ordered a painful mass circumcision.

Then there was the matter of the many thousands of dollars coming into the Temple. Followers were under increasing pressure to make donations and buy certificates in Moses' non-existent silver company (to be redeemed after Judgment Day). There was little evidence that any of this income was going to help the black community, as Moses had promised.

By mid-1981, about twenty dissidents were holding secret meetings. Some of them delved into Moses' past and found hints of scandal. They still believed in his teachings, though, and were looking for ways to reform his movement or perhaps start their own. They included a mechanic, Eric Burke; an accountant, Carlton Carey, and his wife, Mildred; and the Careys' roommate, a cheerful young Jamaican named Aston Green. Moses banned them from the Temple, and demonized them in his sermons. He suggested to his followers that enemies should have their heads cut off.

One evening, Eric Burke drove into the Temple's parking lot. The most hot-headed of the dissidents, he demanded that 'that faggot' Moses come out, and fired a gun into the air before taking off again. Shortly after this, three Yahweh members arrived at the door of Burke's apartment armed with knives. Burke fired some shots through the front door, scaring them away.

The following day, Thursday, 12 November 1981, Aston Green arrived at the Temple and asked to see Moses. He wasn't there, but a group of his enforcers said they would take Green to see him. They led him to a small storage room where they beat him savagely with tire irons, a hammer and other blunt instruments—exactly who and how many took part remains unresolved. Green, barely alive, was put into the trunk of a car and driven to a spot near a quarry at the edge of the Everglades. He was placed in a kneeling position and—after several attempts—his head was severed with a machete.

The corpse was found the next morning. Police identified it from fingerprints, and learned that Green was a Black Hebrew. Some of the dissidents, hearing of his murder through the Temple grapevine, came forward, telling police they feared for their lives. Four of them, including Eric Burke and Carlton Carey, agreed to go to Miami-Dade Police headquarters and make statements that night.

They left the station after 11 p.m. and Carey picked up his wife from a friend's house. Arriving home, they saw a light on in the house. As Carey walked into the living room, wary and carrying a machete, two hooded gunmen burst through a doorway and shot him in the neck. Mildred was shot in the forehead and breast, then one of the men slit her throat. She survived, her husband didn't. His bullet-riddled body was found just outside the back door.

The media reported the victims' links to the Temple of Love. Sister Judith as chief spokesperson angrily denied any involvement. The police interviewed Moses, but with racial tensions always simmering beneath the surface in Florida, were reluctant to take on a black group, and a religious one at that. The other dissidents went into hiding, and no witnesses to the crimes came forward. Eventually, interest in the murders died down.

With his enemies vanquished, Moses celebrated with a new name—Yashua the Messiah—and a bold plan to expand his movement across America.

THE DEATH ⊕F A KARATE EXPERT

Dozens of missionaries in turbans and long white robes traveled across America to set up temples in other cities. At the same time, there was an expansion in the group's commercial activities. As well as the master's books and tapes, they sold T-shirts, hair products, even wine and beer. While recruitment had stalled in Miami, many of the satellite temples were successful. The Nation of Yahweh was growing rich, although little of this money trickled down to its members, who survived on one meal of rice and beans a day. It was also becoming increasingly violent. Anyone seen as lazy or rebellious, or who hadn't raised enough money to meet their daily quota, was subjected to beatings and other punishments. Children were not spared. When his nine-year-old granddaughter, Athalia, was accused of stealing, the Messiah strapped her to a post in the cafeteria, beat her with a stick, and left her there without food for days.

In 1983, twenty-two-year-old Leonard Dupree arrived at the Temple from New Orleans. He was a karate expert who gained a reputation among the others as being a little odd, and some suspected that he was an FBI spy. One day, when he got into an argument with another disciple, others ran to intervene and overpowered him. He was brought to stand before Yashua the Messiah, who asked 'Do you want to challenge me? Challenge me and my brothers?' Dupree said he didn't, but Yashua ordered another Hebrew also skilled in karate, Amri, to come forward. The two men faced each other, and Dupree knocked Amri to the ground. Several men fell upon Dupree, hitting him and tearing off his clothes.

Everyone was screaming. Yashua told Sister Judith to lock the door. He ordered everyone in the room to show their love of God by beating the unbeliever. Around fifty men, women and children swarmed over the body, striking with their fists or whatever weapons came to hand, desperate to get at least one blow in, lest their love of God be questioned. Among them was Jean Mitchell who, despite recent misgivings, remained faithful to her brother. She cried as she remembered the scene years later at his trial. 'They beat his tongue out. They had beat his eyes out ... They crushed his whole body.'

The only two who did not lay a hand on Dupree were Yashua and Sister Judith.

THE EAR MURDERS AND
THE SIEGE ⊕F ⊕PA-L⊕KA

Whatever name he happened to be going by, Hulon Mitchell, Jr. was a fabulously vain individual. He was proud of his pale skin and flashing eyes, which seemed to change color, from blue to yellow to orange, as you looked at them. He told his followers that these attributes had been foretold in the Book of Revelation—which, of course, as God, he had written— when it talked about feet like brass and eyes like 'a flame of fire.'

After the murder of Dupree, he rejoiced. The shared bloodshed had brought his followers closer to him than ever before. He had new robes made, decorated with gold and jewels, and became Yahweh Ben Yahweh. Along with 200 disciples, he set out on a triumphant, twenty-two-city tour. National membership rose to about 5,000.

He now created an inner circle, the price of admission being the killing of a 'white devil.' His men roamed the streets at night in search of easy victims, and returned with an appendage, usually an ear, as proof of their kill. Sometimes the Messiah and others played games with the ears before they were wrapped in newspaper and burned with gasoline.

In May 1986, after an altercation with a gang of youths in Delray Beach, Yahweh Ben Yahweh ordered his men to firebomb an entire block of houses. (As it happened, they accidentally burned the wrong block.) This incident was the catalyst for two former members to go to the FBI, one of whom confessed to taking part in Aston Green's murder. Sickened by the spiraling violence, many others left the Temple of Love, including Jean Mitchell.

Paradoxically, as the group began to fragment internally, it was gaining respectability. Yahweh Ben Yahweh courted Miami's establishment figures, both black and white. He mixed with politicians keen to secure the Yahweh vote. Flush with cash, he bought up rundown buildings and had them refurbished and painted white. The police knew that when the Hebrews moved into an area, the crack dealers and prostitutes moved out.

Yahweh Ben Yahweh learned of a large, decrepit, half-empty apartment complex in the Miami suburb of Opa-loka that seemed perfect for one of his makeovers. The place was a haven for drug dealers and the remaining tenants were at war with the landlords, who refused to spend any more money on it. He made a down payment and, on 28 October 1986, buses full of his enforcers arrived, who told the tenants they would have to move out. Many were single mothers with nowhere else to go, and refused. A standoff ensued, and the police were reluctant to intervene. That night, two tenants who had stood up to the Hebrews, Rudy Broussard and 'Pudley' Brown, were shot dead.

This was, needless to say, something of a PR disaster for Yahweh Ben Yahweh, and he moved quickly to repair the damage. He hired a hotshot white lawyer who told him to drop the racial hatred rhetoric. He opened up the Temple to reporters. His followers threw themselves into urban renewal projects and their acquisition of properties continued, culminating with the purchase of a 106-room resort north of Miami Beach for $1.85 million. The strategy worked and Yahweh Ben Yahweh was hailed as a major businessman and savior to his people. Miami's mayor, Xavier Suarez (whose re-election campaign had received a boost from the Hebrews) proclaimed 7 October 1990 as Yahweh Ben Yahweh Day.

THE ARREST ⊕F G⊕D

Behind the scenes, federal and state authorities were putting together a case against Yahweh Ben Yahweh. They interviewed disciples past and present, including his sister, Jean, who said they would kill for him. 'He may not say, "Go do it," but he takes the mind that way.'

Their most important witness was Bobby Rozier, a former pro footballer whose Yahweh name was Neariah. He had been arrested during the siege at Opa-loka and linked to several crimes, including two of the ear murders. Rozier had, in fact, been the foremost 'death angel,' admitting to six murders for the Messiah (and one for himself). He told them how, after killing a man who had been asleep in his car and cutting off his ear, he had dropped it and been unable to find it, so he cut off the other one. Facing first-degree murder charges, Rozier agreed to testify in return for a reduced sentence.

The investigation dragged on for years. State attorney Janet Reno (who later presided over the fiery deaths of the Branch Davidians at Waco) balked at taking on the case, and insisted it was a federal matter. Finally, a pugnacious assistant U.S. attorney, Richard Scruggs, agreed to handle it.

The FBI planned the arrest of Yahweh Ben Yahweh meticulously. They tracked his every move, waiting for a time when he would be most vulnerable. They feared the Hebrews had weapons and would fight to defend their leader, or perhaps stage a Jonestown-style mass suicide.

On 5 November 1990, Yahweh Ben Yahweh checked into a hotel in New Orleans with a small entourage. In the early hours of the following morning, SWAT teams surrounded the hotel and four Yahweh temples in other cities. An FBI agent rang Yahweh Ben Yahweh's room

185

and told him to come out with his hands up. He asked if he could put on his fancy clothes first, but the agent said no. God, the Son of God was arrested in his bathrobe.

The trial of Yahweh Ben Yahweh and fifteen of his followers on federal charges of conspiracy and racketeering began in January 1992. It was a long, complicated and grueling trial for all concerned. Much of the evidence was harrowing. The prosecution was hampered by the fact that their chief witness, Bobby Rozier, was a self-confessed serial killer. The defendants essentially denied everything, even that some of the murders had taken place. Yahweh Ben Yahweh sat serenely through it all. On the stand he recounted the history of black persecution in America, and read long passages from the Bible.

After four days of deliberation, the jury came to a verdict. Yahweh Ben Yahweh, Sister Judith and five others were convicted of conspiracy. The rest were acquitted, although some were immediately re-arrested by state police on murder charges. At the sentencing, Richard Scruggs asked for the maximum twenty years for Yahweh Ben Yahweh, but the judge took his good works into account and reduced it to eighteen years.

Yahweh Ben Yahweh was found not guilty at a murder trial three months later. The state dropped the other murder charges, which means that none of the murders committed by members of the Nation of Yahweh have ever been prosecuted.

Yahweh Ben Yahweh was released on parole in 2001. He was now a king without a kingdom, one of the conditions of his parole being that he did not meet or communicate electronically with his former followers. When he fell ill with prostate cancer, his lawyers petitioned that these conditions be relaxed so that he could 'die with dignity,' and the request was eventually granted. A few months later, on 7 May 2007, he died in his sleep.

BLOOD
Atonement

Jeffrey Lundgren and
the Kirtland Cult
(Founded 1984)

I had told Dennis Avery what would
happen if he continued to sin, continued
to deny the truth, continued to reject
my teachings, but he continued to
choose darkness rather than light and
he had no-one to blame but himself for
leading himself and his family into this
pit of damnation.

Jeffrey Lundgren

DENNIS AVERY WAS THE FIRST TO DIE. Lured into a barn, jabbed with a stun gun, trussed in duct tape and thrown into a muddy pit 4 feet deep, he was shot twice in the back by Jeffrey Lundgren. His wife, Cheryl, was next, followed by their three daughters, Trina (aged fifteen), Rebecca (thirteen) and Karen (six). The Avery family had been faithful followers of Lundgren, the self-styled Mormon prophet, but in Lundgren's eyes they had sinned, and their slaughter would allow him and his followers to see the face of God.

A PR⊕PHET IN TRAINING

Jeffrey Lundgren and his future wife, Alice Keehler, were born into the Reorganized Church of Jesus Christ of Latter Day Saints, a splinter sect of the much larger and wealthier Church of Jesus Christ of Latter Day Saints, commonly known as the Mormons. The RLDS had its origins in the 1840s, when Brigham Young led most of the Mormons on the great trek west that ended with the foundation of Salt Lake City. A small group stayed behind in Missouri and became the RLDS. Most Mormons believed that Brigham Young was the prophet their founder, Joseph Smith, had predicted would build Zion, the city to which Christ would return. The RLDS believed that prophet was still to come.

Lundgren, born on 3 May 1950, was the son of Don Lundgren, an RLDS elder and ex-navy man. Neither he nor his wife, Lois, showed much affection for their son, who grew up to be a moody young man with few friends. Lundgren courted Alice when they were students at Central Missouri State University. A deeply religious girl, she had been thrilled when an RLDS patriarch prophesied that she would marry a man who would 'do much good unto the children of man' and 'bring forth a marvelous work and wonder.' She became pregnant to Lundgren in 1969 and they were married the following year.

Faced with the draft, Lundgren joined the navy. His ship saw action in Vietnam, coming under bombardment several times, but it was never hit. Lundgren believed that God had saved his life for some special purpose (Alice had told him about the prophecy). He spent much of his spare time memorizing the Mormon scriptures.

Leaving the navy, the Lundgrens lived in California for a while before moving back to Missouri. They had four children, three boys and a girl. The marriage was a deeply troubled one, however. Lundgren rarely had a job, and they were constantly in debt. They survived on the generosity of their parents and friends, and when that failed, Lundgren wrote out bad cheques. His interest in scripture was matched only by his interest in pornography, and he forced a host of extreme sexual practices on Alice, who acquiesced, believing that God had made men the masters. Sometimes Jeffrey beat her and, during one argument, threw her against a wall, injuring her so badly that her spleen had to be removed.

Meanwhile, Lundgren impressed many with his knowledge of the scriptures. In his interpretations, he was a rigid fundamentalist, at odds with the currents of liberalism then flowing through the RLDS. For a while, he taught a Sunday scripture class, until his views became so unorthodox that the church curtailed it. After that, he held classes at his house. Among the regular attendees were two couples, Dennis and Tonya Patrick, who were old friends from university, and Dennis and Cheryl Avery. The Averys were a dowdy, socially awkward pair, devoted to the RLDS but appalled by recent liberal reforms, especially the decision taken at its 1984 conference to allow women priests. Lundgren thought Dennis Avery was a weakling who let his wife boss him around. He mocked them behind their backs, but they were followers, and where would a prophet be without followers?

Then Lundgren received a message from God, telling him to go to Kirtland, a small town in Ohio with a population of about 6,000. Joseph Smith had once received the same message, and while in Kirtland, had built an imposing, two-storey temple. Fortuitously, a job came up as a tour guide there, and Lundgren successfully applied for it. It was unpaid, but a rent-free house was part of the deal, and Lundgren was adept at finding other sources of income.

THE TEMPLE GUIDE

Lundgren became the most enthusiastic guide the Kirtland Temple had ever seen. Its ornate interior was packed with obscure symbolism, and he eagerly set about interpreting it. He was also put in charge of tallying the donations made by visitors. The temple's income began to unaccountably drop.

Lundgren learned of a radical new method of interpreting the scriptures called 'chiasmus,' which involved looking for repetitions. He became convinced that God always spoke using repetitions, and if these weren't immediately apparent to ordinary readers, that was because only God—or one of his prophets—could understand them. Of course, if Lundgren failed to find repetitions in a passage of scripture, that meant it was not the word of God, but of man, and could be ignored. He had found a foolproof system for interpreting scripture any way he liked.

Visions were also coming to him thick and fast. One night, he raced home to tell Alice that he had seen Joseph Smith in the temple. The Mormon founder had smiled at him, and it was a smile of relief—Smith finally had someone who could take over his work. Alice was invariably thrilled to hear of such visions. Sometimes it seemed that she was more desperate for Lundgren to be a prophet than he was.

Lundgren began teaching scripture classes again, and became a hero to Kirtland's fundamentalists, while locking horns with the RLDS's local president, the Reverend Dale Luffman, a liberal. Lundgren's small group of devoted followers included the Patricks and Averys; another couple, Ron and Susie Luff; an old navy buddy, Kevin Currie; and five young RLDS members, Sharon Bluntschly, Danny Kraft, Richard Brand, Greg Winship and Shar Olsen. Lundgren still despised the Averys, but after hearing that Dennis Avery had inherited some money, persuaded them to move to Kirtland. Dennis and his money were soon parted.

Lundgren's skimming of the temple's income eventually came to the notice of church administrators (it was later estimated that he had pocketed more than $20,000) and he was forced to resign. He told his followers that he had been forced out because of his beliefs, and proposed that they form a commune. He rented a two-storey, five-bedroom farmhouse and barn on 15 acres of land, which had previously been an apple orchard. Sharon, Danny, Richard and Shar moved into the farmhouse, where they were soon joined by Lundgren's cousin, Debbie Olivarez. The others all lived nearby. They turned virtually all of their income over to the Lundgrens, or 'Dad' and 'Mom,' as they liked to be called.

193

THE TEMPLE PLⲞT

Lundgren grew bored at the farmhouse. He brooded about losing his job as temple guide. Reading over a passage by Joseph Smith, Jr., he realized that God had given him an order. He and his followers were to take over the temple—by force—and cleanse it of wickedness.

Lundgren had been buying arms and food for a while, in preparation for Armageddon and the return of Christ. By January 1988, planning for the temple raid was under way. Lundgren regaled his followers with the most violent passages in the Bible and the Mormon scriptures, and made them watch such films as *First Blood* and *Apocalypse Now*. They did arms training, and Lundgren built a model of the temple and surrounding buildings for them to study. He had decreed that everyone within a one-block radius of the temple would be killed. The Reverend Dale Luffman, his wife and three children, would be captured and taken into the temple, where Lundgren would behead them. He would then utter a secret prayer. Two days later, a mountain would rise up beneath the temple, an earthquake would destroy the rest of Kirtland, and Christ would appear.

There was only one problem. It had been revealed to Lundgren that the raid should start on 1 May, but not in which year.

Lundgren made it clear that not all his followers would survive the raid. Kevin Currie, whose spirituality Lundgren doubted, realized that he was among those marked for death. Currie, who had left the cult before, left it again. On 28 April, he rang Kirtland's Chief of Police, Dennis Yarborough, and told him about the plot. Currie had previously tried to inform the FBI about it, but the agent he spoke to didn't believe him. Yarborough, however, knew enough about Lundgren to take Currie's story seriously. With 1 May rapidly approaching, he asked Lundgren to come to the police station. When he arrived, Yarborough didn't mention the temple, but said people had been seen undertaking military training on the farm. Lundgren said he didn't know anything about it, but he would keep an eye out. He was clearly rattled.

Soon after this, Lundgren made a trip up the nearby 'mountain' (in fact, more of a hill) where he usually talked to God. He wanted to find out if the raid would take place that year. He returned to say that it was off because of the sinfulness of his followers. He castigated them for it (just as, he said, Jesus had castigated him on the mountain). But then Lundgren had a further revelation that meant that they would not have to take over the temple after all. Instead, killing a number of wicked people in a 'blood atonement' sacrifice would endow him with the necessary power to take them all to see God.

He combed the scriptures to find out who the victims should be.

Yarborough and his men had staked out the farmhouse during the first three nights of May, but of course, nothing had happened. He continued to monitor Lundgren and his group, however. When Shar Olsen defected, Yarborough interviewed her, and she corroborated Currie's story. Dale Luffman also spoke to Olsen, and learned of the plan to behead him. He had Lundgren excommunicated from the RLDS, and delivered the excommunication notice himself. After Luffman left, a thunderstorm occurred, followed by a double rainbow. Lundgren saw this as a sign that God had opened the first of the 'seven seals' that, according to The Book of Revelation, must be opened before Christ can return. He told the others that the human sacrifice would open the second seal. When that had been done, they would travel into the wilderness, where he would figure out how to open the remaining seals.

Further study of the scriptures revealed to Lundgren that the wicked people he was to sacrifice would come from his own 'house.' That could only mean the Averys.

SACRIFICE

On 17 April, the Averys, who had stopped attending Lundgren's regular classes (another sign of their wickedness), were invited to dinner at the farmhouse. After dinner, Alice took her three youngest children out shopping. Lundgren gathered Ron Luff, Richard Brand, Danny Kraft, Greg Winship and Damon, his eldest son, in his bedroom. He looked them all in the eye and said, 'Are you in or are you out?' They all said they were in.

Ron Luff, who had become Lundgren's second-in-command, told Dennis Avery that the prophet wanted to see him in the barn. As Dennis entered it, Luff pulled a stun gun from his pocket and jabbed him with it several times, but it didn't incapacitate him. Dennis was overpowered, and duct tape was wrapped around his hands, feet and mouth. He was dragged to the back of the barn, where a pit had been laboriously dug in the hard, wet earth. Greg Winship was outside, firing up a chain saw that would mask the sound of gunfire. Lundgren, left alone with Dennis, stood over the pit with a .45 pistol in his hand. Dennis had managed to get onto his knees when Lundgren shot him. When he had finished, he called the other men in. 'Come and see what death is.'

Luff brought out Cheryl next. She was also bound with duct tape, laid beside her husband's corpse and shot, as was their eldest daughter, Trina. Rebecca, lured in by the prospect of seeing horses, was the only one to put up a struggle, but she was quickly subdued.

Finally, Luff gave six-year-old Karen a piggyback into the barn. As Lundgren killed each of them, he experimented with different guns and bullets, and shooting them in different places—he shot Karen through the top of the skull. The scriptures had told him he would have to kill again, so he needed to become good at it. When the Averys were all dead, their bodies were sprinkled with lime, the pit was filled in, and the area was strewn with rubbish.

A cynic might observe that Lundgren had managed to fulfil one of his fantasies about the temple raid—the brutal murder of a couple and their three children—in a manner that posed much less danger to his own skin.

The following day, Dennis Yarborough and his men, accompanied by FBI agents, raided the farm. They questioned everyone and Lundgren showed them some of their guns, but they didn't have a search warrant and couldn't find anything illegal. They left, frustrated.

'THE G⊕D ⊕F THE WH⊕LE EARTH'

As soon as the police and FBI had left, Lundgren's followers began to pack for their trip to the wilderness. Lundgren left first, and headed for West Virginia. A few days later, they had gathered in an isolated valley in the Appalachian Mountains, where they set up tents. They now numbered twenty-four men, women and children, including an old college friend of Lundgren's, Keith Johnson, and his wife, Kathy. They had joined a month before—in time for Keith to help dig the pit in the barn.

Lundgren climbed another mountain, and came back with exciting news. Jesus was very happy about the slaughter of the Averys, and had bestowed upon him a new title—'The God of the Whole Earth.' He was also now immortal.

The only member of the group who seemed to be affected by the murders was Dennis Patrick, who fell into a deep depression. Lundgren was infuriated that he wouldn't accept God's commandments. He threatened to kill Dennis. Then he relented, but said that Dennis' wife, Tonya, and daughter, Molly, had to move into his tent. After a few days, he told Tonya that God intended her to be his second wife. Alice violently objected to this, but Lundgren said God had made it all quite clear. He was to pierce Tonya one way or another, and whether he did it with a bullet or his penis was up to Alice. She was forced to relent.

Lundgren tired of Tonya almost immediately. He accused her of sinfulness. In fact, he said, the sinfulness of all the women was the group's main problem. But he had a solution. The women could relinquish their sins by stripping off their clothes and dancing in front of him. While they did this he would masturbate, and finish by ejaculating into their panties. God equated blood with semen, Lundgren explained, so it would be the equivalent of Christ shedding his blood on the cross.

Over two days, Susie, Sharon, Kathy and Debbie all stripped for Jeffrey in his tent, dancing to tapes of his favorite songs as Alice sat beside him. Having seen them all perform, and taken their sins onto himself, Jeffrey decided that he had made a mistake about Tonya, and it was actually Kathy who was supposed to be his second wife. Alice, who hated Kathy, couldn't accept this. She fled to her parents' house.

At this point, the group began to fragment. Richard Brand and Greg Winship left. The onset of winter forced the others to abandon their forest retreat, and they ended up living in a barn owned by Ron Luff's brother, Rick. When Rick discovered that Lundgren was practicing polygamy, he ordered him out. Lundgren didn't care. He had told Alice he was sick of his followers, and went to California to recruit some new ones.

With Lundgren gone, the others scattered. One by one they lost their faith in him as a prophet. They knew they were all culpable for the murders, but if they didn't say anything, Lundgren would surely kill again. Keith Johnson was the first to break ranks, and in December 1989 told investigators about the bodies in the barn. They were exhumed, and Jeffrey and Alice were arrested in San Diego.

Alice, who was tried first, used 'battered wife syndrome' as a defence. She said she had not known that the Averys were to be killed. The jury didn't believe her. She was found guilty of conspiring to commit aggravated murder, and sentenced to 150 years in prison.

At his trial, Lundgren addressed the jury for five hours prior to sentencing. He went through the scriptures and defended all his actions. 'Prophets have been asked by the lord to go forth and kill since the beginning of time,' he told them. He was sentenced to death.

All the other men who had actively taken part in the murders received long sentences.

Jeffrey Lundgren spent his years on death row studying the scriptures and launching various appeals. On 17 October 2006, a stay of execution was granted after he claimed that, because he had become so obese in prison, death by lethal injection would be particularly painful and constitute cruel and unusual punishment. An appeals court rejected this, and on 26 October, the 'God of the Whole Earth' was put to death.

Modern
KNIGH+S
+EMPLAR

The Order of the
Solar Temple

(Founded 1984)

Liberation is not where human beings
think it is. Death can represent an
essential stage of life.

Luc Jouret

THE KNIGHTS TEMPLAR, FOUNDED IN THE EARLY TWELFTH CENTURY, were an order of Christian knights dedicated to protecting pilgrims in the Holy Land. Over two centuries, they amassed great wealth and became in effect the international bankers of the day. While famed for their exploits during the Crusades, they were despised by some for their greed and arrogance. In 1307, King Philip IV of France ordered all Templars arrested, and urged his fellow European rulers to do the same. While Philip may have had genuine fears that the Templars (who owed their allegiance to the Pope) had political ambitions, it's more likely he was after their money. The Vatican joined in the persecution and the Templars were charged with heresy. Under torture, members confessed to having Islamic sympathies and links to the dreaded sect of Assassins, worshipping a severed head called Baphomet, and renouncing Christ in a ceremony during which they spat on a cross. In 1314, the Templar Grand Master, Jacques de Molay, was roasted on a spit and the order officially abolished. But the Western world has never really been able to let the Templars go. One enduring belief, held by many conspiracy theorists, is that the Templars simply went underground, only to emerge later as the Freemasons.

Over the years, many groups have evoked the Templars and claimed to carry on their traditions. One of the most interesting, and mysterious, was the Order of the Solar Temple, a cult that self-destructed in spectacular fashion before many had even heard of it.

THE D⊕UBLE ACT

Much about the history, structure and membership of the Order of the Solar Temple remains obscure. Nevertheless, its development under its chief instigator,

Joseph Di Mambro, and younger charismatic leader, Luc Jouret, can be sketched in broad terms.

Di Mambro was born on 19 August 1924 in southern France, and became a jeweler. He developed an interest in esoteric subjects, and in 1956 joined the Ancient and Mystical Order Rosae Crucis (AMORC), otherwise know as the Rosicrucians. This is one of several groups claiming to be the continuation of the original Rosicrucians, a Christian mystical movement dating back to the early seventeenth century (AMORC was actually founded in the United States in 1915). Di Mambro began another career as a con man and bogus psychiatrist, and was forced to leave France after allegations were raised against him. He went to Switzerland, where he was charged with fraud and passing bad cheques. Returning to France in 1972, he founded the Center for the Preparation for the New Age, and opened a commune near the Swiss border. He expected his followers, many of them former Rosicrucians, to donate all their wealth to his new order. He arranged marriages for them and decided who could have children. He said that nine 'cosmic children' would be born who would help bring about a new age. The most important of these was his daughter, Emmanuelle, who was the new messiah.

Some of Di Mambro's followers were wealthy, and in 1976 he was able to buy a fifteen-room mansion in Geneva. In 1978, he founded a new, secret order, the Golden Way. It was around this time that he met Luc Jouret.

Jouret was born on 17 October 1947 in the Belgian Congo. He studied medicine at the Free University in Brussels, graduating in 1974. Jouret distrusted modern medicine, however. He studied homeopathy, and on a trip to the Philippines, became fascinated by faith healing. He married a woman named Marie-Christine and they had a son, who died four days after birth. The marriage ended soon afterwards.

Jouret joined Di Mambro's Golden Way and another organization, the Renewed Order of the Temple. This had grown out of the Sovereign Order of the Solar Temple, founded in 1952 by a French writer, Jacques Breyer, and was led by Julien Origas, who was said to have been a former Gestapo or SS officer. After the death of Origas in 1983, Jouret tried to take over the leadership of this group, but was forced out, taking half its membership with him.

According to some accounts, before meeting Jouret, Di Mambro had been looking for a charismatic individual to be the front man for his organization. Jouret, with his charm, good looks and medical credentials, fitted the bill perfectly. In 1984, Di Mambro and Jouret founded the International Chivalric Organization of the Solar Tradition, which was later renamed the Order of the Solar Temple.

STRUCTURE, BELIEFS AND RITUALS

Jouret traveled through France, Switzerland and Canada, giving lectures and holding seminars. He spoke on such topics as 'Medicine and Conscience,' and the ideals he espoused were lofty ones, combining Christianity with new-age beliefs. Humanity was going through a period of transition, he said. The purpose of his group was to aid this transformation by reaffirming the primacy of the spiritual over the temporal, and bringing all churches together. There was also an apocalyptic tone to his lectures. Earth was in great danger from pollution and other environmental disasters, and was about to suffer some sort of terrible cataclysm.

The Solar Temple had a complicated structure. When Jouret gave public lectures, he spoke as a representative of the Amenta Club. Anyone who seemed interested was asked to join the Archedia Club, in which they participated in rituals and learned more of the group's beliefs. Finally, those deemed worthy—and wealthy—enough were invited to join a secret inner circle, the Order of the Solar Temple. Once initiated, they were expected to donate much of their income to the group, and pledge complete subservience to its leaders. Di Mambro claimed that the ultimate leaders of the Solar Temple were thirty-three 'Elder Brothers' who lived in Zurich and were called 'the Synarchy,' but there is no evidence that they existed.

Di Mambro and Jouret claimed to have been Knights Templar in previous lives, and Di Mambro used a sword in rituals that he said was a genuine Templar artifact. As in most secret societies, initiates progressed through various levels as they advanced spiritually (although, in the Solar Temple's case, advancement seems to have depended more on how much money the initiate had donated). The three levels were called 'The Brothers of Parvis,' 'The Knights of the Alliance' and 'The Brothers of the Ancient Times,' and each of these levels was subdivided into three grades. Solar Temple lodges had a room set aside for rituals, with an altar and other religious paraphernalia. As they ascended the hierarchy, members had to spend large sums of money on Templar-style robes and jewelry. Those who had reached the highest level wore gold capes.

The Solar Temple's doctrines regarding death and the end of the world were somewhat contradictory and changed over time. In early tapes and lectures, Jouret indicated that Temple members constituted an elect who would survive the apocalypse, which would involve a 'purifying' fire, and usher in the age of Aquarius. The group published literature telling its members how to survive in the event of nuclear, chemical or biological warfare, and underground shelters were dug on Temple properties. After their move to Canada, Jouret claimed that Quebec would be the only place that would survive the apocalypse. Over the years, however, practical preparations for the end of the world gave way to the idea that the Temple's members might have to leave this world—by dying—before the end came. Jouret told his followers that death was illusory, and when they died their spirits would travel to a planet that orbited Sirius, also known as the Dog Star, which has long figured in esoteric beliefs. He suggested that to achieve this, their deaths would have to come by fire, just like many of the the original Templars.

PARAN⊕IA

In 1986, Di Mambro and Jouret moved their headquarters to Canada. They bought a chalet complex in Morin Heights, Quebec, and established a center in the tourist town of Sainte-Anne-de-la-Pérade.

By 1989, the Solar Temple had more than 400 members, mostly in France, Switzerland, Canada and Martinique, with a handful in the United States and Spain. Because of the group's recruiting methods, these people tended to be older than the members of most cults, and many were professionals. They included Robert Ostiguy, the mayor of Richelieu, in Quebec; Camille Pilet, a former international sales manager for the Swiss watchmaker Piaget; Jocelyne Grand-Maison, a journalist; and Robert Falardeau, a department chief in Quebec's Ministry of Finance. The Temple's income during its existence has been estimated at close to $100 million, and Di Mambro owned some eighty properties in France, Switzerland, Australia and Martinique.

In the early 1990s, cracks began to appear. Jouret's behavior became more excessive, and he regularly had sex with female members before rituals, supposedly to increase his 'spiritual energy.' This resulted in the break up of several marriages, and a few long-standing members left. The group was also facing media scrutiny for the first time. A Canadian anti-cult organization took an interest in it, and encouraged a former member, Rose-Marie Klaus, to go to the press. Solar Temple leaders became paranoid, and started to stockpile weapons. In 1993, two members were arrested for gun dealing and illegal possession of firearms, and a warrant was issued for Jouret. By then he had fled to Switzerland.

Di Mambro had his own problems. He was being investigated in several countries on suspicion of money laundering and other crimes. He was suffering from diabetes and other ailments, and reportedly believed he had cancer. And his family was in revolt. His 'cosmic' daughter Emmanuelle, who had been brought up in isolation from the outside world, turned twelve in 1994, and was demanding to lead a normal life. His son Elie had already left the group in disgust, having discovered that some of the apparently paranormal events that took place during Temple rituals, including the appearance of ghostly figures, images of the Holy Grail and so on, had been faked by Di Mambro using hidden projectors. About fifteen others left after Elie's departure.

Another follower who was becoming disillusioned was Tony Dutoit. He and his English-born wife, Nicky, had close links to the Temple's leaders in Switzerland. Nicky made some of the robes that members wore in rituals, and was Emmanuelle Di Mambro's governess. When Dutoit became curious about Di Mambro's finances, he and his wife were packed off to Quebec, where he publicly admitted to helping install the projectors and other electronic devices Di Mambro used during rituals. The revelations of such blatant fraud posed a severe threat to the Solar Temple's existence. In addition to this, the Dutoits had angered Di Mambro by naming their newborn son Christopher Emmanuel (thus appropriating Di Mambro's daughter's name). Di Mambro told his followers that the Dutoits' baby was the Antichrist.

On 4 October 1994, a fire broke out in the Dutoits' condominium in Morin Heights. After it was extinguished, five bodies were found inside. Tony Dutoit had been stabbed fifty times in the back. Nicky had been stabbed in the throat, back and breast. Three-month-old Christopher Emmanuel had been stabbed six times with a wooden stake. A plastic bag had been placed over his head and his body had been stuffed behind a heater. In a bedroom upstairs, the bodies of a man and a woman were found. These would later be identified as Solar Temple members Gerry and Collette Genoud. Firebombs attached to timer mechanisms had been placed in the rooms, and bin liners full of petrol hung from doorknobs.

As the Quebec police puzzled over this bizarre crime scene, word came through of even stranger events in Switzerland.

THE TRANSIT T⊕ SIRIUS

About twelve hours after the Quebec fire started, a farmhouse in Cheiry, Switzerland, was seen to be ablaze. Firemen found the body of the owner, a Solar Temple member named Albert Giacobino, lying on a bed with a plastic bag over his head.

Searching the house later, investigators found incendiary devices scattered around it. In a building next to it, apparently used as a meeting hall, they found a secret door leading to a semi-basement area divided into three rooms. One was set up as a chapel, with a red carpet, red satin hangings and an altar. Around this, eighteen bodies were arranged in a star shape, their feet closest to the altar. They wore ceremonial robes and capes of red, white, black and gold. Four more bodies were found in the other rooms. Many of the bodies had plastic bags over their heads, and some had their hands bound. Autopsies revealed that most had been shot in the head, some more than once, and three had been suffocated. As in Quebec, incendiary devices and bin liners full of petrol had been scattered though the buildings, but those within the secret rooms had failed to ignite. There were empty Champagne bottles on the floor.

Firefighters were still battling the blaze at Cheiry when, about 100 miles away in the village of Salvan, three chalets owned by the Solar Temple were also burning. Twenty-five bodies in sleeping bags were found inside, burned beyond recognition. The victims had been drugged and most of them shot.

An international manhunt for Luc Jouret began, with reports suggesting he had fled to Australia, but on 13 October, Swiss authorities announced that his body was among those found at Salvan, along with Joseph Di Mambro, his daughter Emmanuelle, and other leading members of the Solar Temple.

In the days following the fires, a number of 'testament' letters were received by journalists, government officials and other parties. (These had been posted by a young Temple member, Patrick Vuarnet, who had been entrusted with them by Di Mambro just before his death.) The letters denounced the persecution by the Canadian government, and affirmed that Solar Temple members had voluntarily embarked on their transit to Sirius. 'We have planned in a full state of consciousness, without any fanaticism, our transit which has nothing to do with suicide in the human meaning of the word,' said one. The letters also stated that there were traitors in their midst who would 'suffer the punishment they deserve for the ages of the ages.'

Canadian police determined that the Dutoits had been murdered by two Solar Temple members, Joel Egger and Dominique Bellaton (the mother of Di Mambro's daughter Emmanuelle) on 30 September. The two other Temple members whose bodies were found in the condominium, Gerry and Collette Genoud, had been drugged, and apparently went to their deaths willingly (autopsies showed they were alive when the fires started). Egger and Bellaton left the condominium on the evening of 3 October, having set the incendiary devices to ignite at 5 a.m. They caught a plane to Switzerland, arriving on the morning of 4 October. Later that day, Di Mambro and Jouret were seen in a supermarket in Salvan, buying a large number of plastic bin liners.

The exact sequence of events after that will never be known. Some of the forty-eight who died in Switzerland (including seven children and teenagers) and an unknown number of 'traitors,' were clearly murdered. Others may have submitted to being killed. The Swiss inquest into the deaths concluded that only fifteen people had committed suicide. It is not known who carried out the killings, but it is suspected that Egger and Bellaton took part (their bodies were found at Salvan). Another mystery is an apparent last-minute falling out between Di Mambro and Jouret. Among the letters given to Patrick Vuarnet to post was a note from Di Mambro in which he wrote, 'Following tragic transit at Cheiry, we insist on specifying, in the name of the Rose+Cross, that we deplore and totally dissociate ourselves from the barbarous, incompetent and aberrant conduct of Doctor Luc Jouret ... the cause of a veritable carnage which could have been a transit performed in Honour, Peace and Light.'

Both Di Mambro's estranged son Elie and Jouret's ex-wife Marie-Christine were among the dead at Salvan. It seems they may have been lured there to exact revenge.

MORE SURPRISES

'The Rose+Cross has definitely not finished surprising you,' stated one of the Solar Temple's final letters, which proved prophetic. On the evening of 23 December 1995 (the winter solstice), the burned bodies of sixteen members were found in a chalet near Grenoble, France. Among them were a former French Olympic skier turned sunglasses tycoon, Jean Vuarnet, his wife Emily and son Patrick. The victims had been drugged and shot, and their bodies laid out in a star pattern. On 22 March 1997 (the summer solstice), the bodies of a further five members were found in a burned-out house in Quebec.

Only one person has been brought to a court on charges relating to the deaths. This was a Swiss musician and former conductor for the Canadian Opera Company, Michael Tabachnik, who went on trial in France in 2001. The charges focused on his alleged role in the deaths of the sixteen members in 1995. Prosecutors argued that Tabachnik was a leading member who had been present at meetings where the murders and suicides were planned. He was acquitted due to a lack of evidence. Prosecutors appealed and Tabachnik was again put on trial in October 2006, but was once again cleared of all charges.

While little has been heard from the group since 1997, it is believed it still has several hundred members in Canada and Europe. Further surprises cannot be ruled out.

Engineering
ARMAGEDDON

Aum Shinrikyo
(Founded 1987)

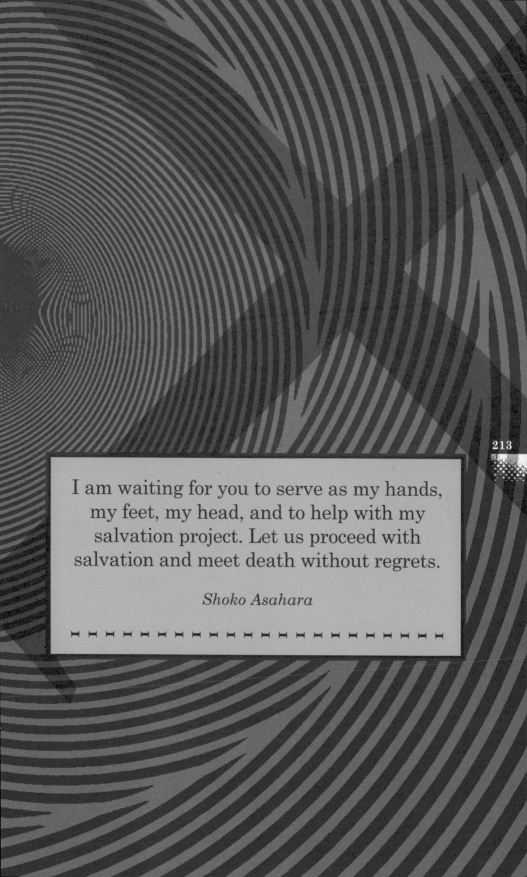

I am waiting for you to serve as my hands, my feet, my head, and to help with my salvation project. Let us proceed with salvation and meet death without regrets.

Shoko Asahara

ON THE MORNING OF **20 MARCH 1995**, five men boarded separate trains on the Tokyo subway system. Each carried an umbrella and a package wrapped in newspaper. Inside the packages were plastic bags containing a liquid solution of the nerve gas sarin.

As 8 a.m. approached, the trains converged on Kasumigaseki, where the offices of many Japanese government ministries are located. The men placed their packages on the floor beneath their seats and punctured them with the tips of their umbrellas, which had been sharpened for this purpose. They left the trains hurriedly as the liquid began to leak out, evaporate and spread through the carriages.

The men were members of Aum Shinrikyo, a 40,000-strong cult led by the almost-blind guru Shoko Asahara. Aum publicly espoused Buddhist ideals of the sacredness of life—its members were forbidden to kill so much as a cockroach. Yet Asahara and his chief lieutenants followed a different morality, in which killing people meant raising them to a higher spiritual level. Many cult leaders have predicted the end of the world, but Asahara is the only one who actively sought the means to bring it about.

THE MOUNTAIN WIZARD

Shoko Asahara was born Chizuo Matsumoto in Kyushu, Japan, on 2 March 1955. The son of a straw-mat weaver, he was born with glaucoma which left him partially sighted in one eye and blind in the other. (Although some have claimed that he exaggerated his blindness—on at least one occasion he was seen driving a car.) He went to a school for the blind, where his partial sight enabled him to bully other pupils. Fiercely ambitious, he dreamed of making a fortune and perhaps becoming prime minister, but failed Tokyo University's entrance exam. He married a girl named Tomoko in 1978 and, with money from her parents, started an acupuncture and yoga clinic with a sideline in dubious herbal remedies. He was amazed by the amounts of money that people were willing to pay for these. Previously uninterested in religion, he began to study it in earnest. He gave his organization the fantastic title of Aum Association of Mountain Wizards, 'Aum' being the sacred Hindu word (sometimes written as 'om') which encapsulates the universe.

Japan was experiencing a boom in alternative religions at this time, with hundreds of new groups appearing each year. Matsumoto joined a Buddhist sect called Agonshu, which taught that enlightenment could be gained through meditation and monetary offerings. He was an impatient man, however. In 1986, he went to India where, in time-honored fashion, he sat on a mountain in the Himalayas and found enlightenment by himself. On a return visit the following year, he managed to have his photo taken with the Dalai Lama who, according to Matsumoto, told him that he had 'the mind of a real Buddha,' and had a mission in Japan. The Dalai Lama later disputed this conversation.

Matsumoto, now calling himself Shoko Asahara (shoko means 'bright light'), said enlightenment had given him supernatural powers, including telepathy, X-ray vision and the ability to levitate. His claims received wide publicity in the Japanese media, and he opened more clinics. His organization began to take on a much more religious tone. He put together a theology incorporating bits of Buddhism, Hinduism, various new-age beliefs, the prophecies of Nostradamus (a great fad in Japan during the 1970s) and the apocalyptic visions of the Book of Revelation. He renamed his movement Aum Shinrikyo (Aum Supreme Truth).

215

Asahara settled easily into the role of a god in human form. His hair and beard clippings were available to devotees—for a price. For $800, they could have some of his used bathwater, while a 'Blood Initiation,' in which the devotee was given a small glass of the master's blood to drink, cost $7000. The latter was guaranteed to bestow magical powers.

Aum recruited aggressively and membership soon exceeded 1,000. Those wishing to become full-time 'renunciates' had to sign over all they owned to Aum and cut ties with their families. The money poured in, and construction of the group's headquarters, a sprawling compound at the foot of Mount Fuji, began in 1988. The following year, despite the strenuous objections of some parents whose children had joined, Aum was granted official status as a religion.

Aum's recruits tended to be young and highly educated, with many having a scientific background. Physicists, engineers, doctors, electronics experts and computer programmers seemed particularly susceptible to Asahara's promises of perfect health and superpowers, and Asahara was eager to harness their technical skills. The cult's hi-tech bent was most visible in the electronic cap, called a PSI (for Perfect Salvation Initiation), that many members wore on their heads. Developed by Aum's chief scientist, Hideo Murai, the cap supposedly adjusted the brainwaves of its wearer so that they matched those of the guru. (Asahara, according to Aum's doctors, had reached such a state of enlightenment that his brainwaves registered virtually nothing on an electroencephalogram.) The caps, which resembled bandages threaded with multicolored wires, were rented out to followers for $700 a month, and brought in a huge amount of money.

The life of most Aum members was strictly regimented. They worked long hours, ate meager rations of rice and boiled vegetables, and got by on little more than three hours' sleep. Anyone who broke the rules, including the strict rule enforcing celibacy, faced punishments such as solitary confinement, or suspension by their feet. Nevertheless, many later claimed that they had enjoyed and benefited spiritually from this harsh routine.

Life for the guru was rather different. Asahara gorged himself on rich foods until he became obese. He lived separately from his wife and six children, in luxurious quarters equipped with a bath big enough for ten people. Young female members regularly disappeared into these quarters for special 'initiations.' It was sometimes said within Aum that, to rise in the group's spiritual hierarchy, one had to be a graduate of Tokyo University—or an attractive young woman.

THE FIRST ᙏURDERS

In 1988, a twenty-one-year-old Aum member, Shuji Taguchi, told people that he wanted to leave. He was disappointed that the promised enlightenment had failed to eventuate, and unnerved by the death of another member who, expressing similar misgivings, had been subjected to dunking in near freezing water. Word of Taguchi's intentions reached the cult's leaders, and he was imprisoned in a tiny cell. When he continued to insist that he wanted out, he was strangled by Murai and four others. His body was burned and the ashes scattered.

Later that year, a Yokohama human rights lawyer, Tsutsumi Sakamoto, began to take on the cases of parents who were trying to extract their children from Aum. Others who had fled and wanted their money back also sought him out, and he ended up founding the Society for Aum Shinrikyo Victims. Such organized opposition was too much for Asahara, who told some of his most trusted lieutenants that Sakamoto must be eliminated.

One night in November 1989, six Aum members, including Murai and a doctor, Tomomasa Nakagawa, arrived at Sakamoto's house. Inside, the lawyer, his wife, Satoko, and fourteen-month-old son were sleeping. The boy woke as they entered the house, and was given a deadly injection of potassium chloride by Nakagawa. Sakamoto, who put up a fierce struggle, was bludgeoned, injected with poison and eventually strangled, as was Satoko.

The bodies were buried in three separate locations, after the teeth of the lawyer and his wife had been removed to prevent identification.

The media were quick to suspect Aum's involvement in the family's disappearance (the killers had hidden their tracks well, so there was no proof that they had been murdered). The local police were inexperienced in murder cases, however, and reluctant to investigate a religious group. Eventually, interest in the case died down. Over the next few years, as Aum grew more powerful and its intentions more deadly, the failure of the Japanese police to investigate it would become increasingly baffling.

PREPARING F⊕R WAR

Asahara decided that Aum would contest the 1993 elections for the Japanese parliament, the Diet. It fielded twenty-five candidates and spent millions of dollars on the campaign, which saw hundreds of followers take to the streets wearing papier-mâché masks of Asahara's pudgy, bearded face. They were all genuinely dismayed when the campaign was a dismal failure. It was a big setback for Aum, and many members left. Asahara grew increasingly scathing about contemporary society, and his warnings about an imminent apocalypse became even more strident.

Asahara had long predicted the end of the world. The details and dates kept changing, but the scenario included a war between Japan and the United States, Japan sinking beneath the sea, and a global nuclear war that would destroy civilization. Like most doomsday prophets, Asahara taught that only those who followed him would survive. His particular twist was to claim that the spiritual purity of Aum members would make them impervious to radiation, poisons and other physical threats. In addition to this, Aum would not just be a passive witness to Armageddon, but an active participant. Asahara wanted nothing less than to turn Aum into an army. And an army needs weapons.

Far from being put off by such a scenario, Aum's scientists and technicians virtually fell over each other trying to help achieve it. Their initial efforts involved the development of biological weapons. Seichi Endo, a biologist formerly with Kyoto University, was put in charge of a program to cultivate large quantities of botulinum bacteria, which causes botulism and is one of the most toxic naturally occurring substances. Their first attempt at using it came in April 1990, when a specially-equipped vehicle was driven through the streets around the Diet, spraying botulinum into the air. There were no reports of illnesses, however, and a second attempt at spreading botulism, during the wedding of Prince Naruhito in 1993, also failed. Abandoning botulism, Endo turned his attentions to anthrax, and a laboratory for producing it was set up in an eight-storey building in Tokyo. In an experiment lasting four days, anthrax vapor was pumped into the air from the roof. Plants wilted, pets became sick and there was a foul stench in the air, but again no people fell ill—it seems Endo may have used a strain of the bacterium not harmful to humans.

While these experiments were being carried out, Aum was seeking other weapons of mass destruction. The opportunities to obtain them increased with the cult's rapid and unexpected expansion into Russia. Asahara had embarked on a 'Russian Salvation Tour' in 1992, during which he had met the vice president, donated $80,000 worth of computers to the Moscow State University, and addressed 19,000 people in Moscow's Olympic stadium. Aum poured a huge amount of money into its Russian recruiting drive, and its message proved peculiarly attractive there. When Aum reached its peak, with 40,000 members in 1995, three-quarters of them were in Russia.

Kiyohide Hayakawa, was in charge of developing the infrastructure needed to wage war. He was Aum's 'Minister of Construction.' He made numerous trips to Russia, where he cultivated contacts in the military and with scientists formerly involved in the Soviet Union's chemical and biological weapons programs. He sought to buy lasers, rocket launchers, helicopters, fighter planes, tanks and even nuclear warheads. Aum certainly had the cash to buy such hardware. As well as the millions that flowed in from its Russian followers, it had bought a huge amount of property cheaply during Japan's recession, and its businesses there were booming. It owned computer shops, a chain of restaurants and other lucrative ventures. With its employees basically working for free, and the tax breaks afforded a religious institution, Aum could hardly go wrong.

Aum members were now spending much of their time doing military training. A sophisticated manufacturing plant, known as the Supreme Science Institute, was established 20 miles from Mount Fuji to supply them with weapons. An AK-74 automatic rifle smuggled out of Russia was used as a prototype, and Asahara ordered that 1,000 of them, along with a million bullets, be made by the end of 1995.

Aum also remained committed to developing biological and chemical agents, and chief chemist Masami Tsutchiya had come up with a new idea.

SARIN THE BRAVE

Sarin is a nerve gas developed by the Nazis, although the war ended before they had a chance to mass-produce it. A tiny drop of it is enough to kill a human being. The symptoms of sarin poisoning include nausea, difficulty in breathing, a contraction of the pupils (so that the world appears to have gone dark), loss of control over bodily functions, and convulsions, after which the victim may fall into a coma and die.

A three-storey warehouse in the Mount Fuji compound, known as Satyam No. 7, was set aside for the mass production of sarin. Aum spent $10 million installing reactors, pipes and huge steel vats full of chemicals (all without attracting the attention of the notoriously incurious Japanese authorities). Amid all this, in a touch worthy of a James Bond villain, was a golden image of Asahara's favorite deity, Shiva, the Hindu god of destruction. Access to Satyam No. 7 was restricted to a few trusted Aum members. One of them recalled that 'a strange, whitish mist' hung in the air, and that everyone who worked there got sick. To cheer themselves as they worked, they sang a rousing song that went in part:

> **It came from Nazi Germany, a dangerous little chemical weapon**
> **Sarin! Sarin!**
> **If you inhale the mysterious vapor, you will fall with bloody vomit from your mouth**
> **Sarin! Sarin! Sarin—**
> **the chemical weapon.**
> **Song of Sarin, the brave.**

Tsutchiya perfected the manufacture of sarin at the end of 1993. It was decided to test it at Banjawarn Station, a 500,000-acre sheep station in Western Australia purchased earlier that year because of its uranium deposits (Aum's scientists had been toying with the idea of making their own nuclear weapons). A quantity of sarin was released into the air at Banjawarn, and a herd of 24 sheep convulsed and died.

Asahara was excited about his new weapon, and keen to see it used on people. An opportunity came up during a dispute over property that Aum had bought in the resort town of Matsumoto, Japan. The dispute went to court and, when it looked like the judgment would go against Aum, it was decided to delay it by poisoning the three judges.

On the evening of 27 June 1994, a refrigerated truck was parked near the Matsumoto courthouse. Inside it were six Aum members and 44 pounds of sarin. The gas was pumped through a window of the truck and wafted through the town, killing seven people and injuring hundreds of others. The judges escaped death thanks to a change in the wind direction. Local police did not suspect Aum, instead coming up with a ridiculous theory that one of the victims, a salesman named Kono, had accidentally made sarin while mixing herbicide in his garden.

THE SOLDIERS OF WHITE LOVE

Asahara was now preaching that Armageddon would begin with Aum mounting a successful coup against the Japanese government. Its army, 'the Soldiers of White Love,' including troops from Russia, would invade Japan. At the same time, Aum helicopters would fly over Tokyo, pumping out sarin and incapacitating the government. Aum would triumph, and Asahara would be crowned the 'Holy Monk Emperor.' It was all due to begin in November 1995.

How could anyone think that such an insane plan could work? Part of the answer probably lies in the enormous quantities of drugs being taken by Aum members. Asahara had first tried LSD in early 1994 and become convinced of its spiritual uses. With its usual zeal, Aum began to mass produce it, along with a host of other drugs, including methamphetamines, PCP (phencyclidine, also known as angel dust) and sodium thiopental (better known as truth serum), and these were regularly given to members, as part of rituals or slipped into their meals. This can only have contributed to the paranoia of the group, who already believed that government planes and helicopters regularly flew over the Mount Fuji compound to spray poison gas on them.

After numerous complaints had been received about foul chemical odors emanating from Aum properties, the Japanese police were finally taking an interest in Aum.

The cult had also perpetrated two particularly brazen crimes: attempting to kill an investigative journalist, Shoko Egawa, by pumping phosgene gas through her door; and the kidnap and murder of a sixty-eight-year-old notary whose wealthy sister had fled from Aum. On 1 January 1995, a newspaper reported that police had found sarin residue in the soil around the Mount Fuji compound. Asahara panicked and ordered Satyam No.7 be cleaned up. Thousands of gallons of chemicals were dumped down drains, and the building was hastily disguised as a 'shrine' complete with an enormous Styrofoam Buddha. Aum held press conferences, denouncing religious persecution.

A massive earthquake in Kobe later that month (which Asahara, of course, claimed to have predicted) stalled the police investigation, but only temporarily. Aum members who had infiltrated the police reported that raids were planned for 21 March. Asahara decided to attack first.

AP⊕CALYPSE N⊕W

The plan worked almost perfectly, aided by the precision timing of the Tokyo subway. Five Aum members were able to release their sarin gas. As commuters staggered from carriages, coughing, their eyes stinging and noses running, the trains moved on, spreading the gas to other stations. Confused messages came over loudspeakers. Hundreds emerged from subway exits and collapsed on the streets. Others staggered on to work, only to discover from TV reports that they had been gassed.

In all, twelve people died as a direct result of the attack, and more than 5,500 were affected. Many hundreds still suffer the physical after-effects, including headaches, nausea and poor vision, while some have developed post-traumatic stress disorder.

The attack sent a wave of panic through Japan. As usual, Aum came out swinging, denying any involvement and claiming that it was they who were under attack from the U.S. military. On 22 March, 1,000 police in protective suits raided the Mount Fuji compound and began to uncover Aum's incredible stockpile of chemical and other weapons. It was later estimated that they had the capacity to make enough sarin to kill four million people. Meanwhile there were a number of further attacks, with packages containing hydrogen chloride left in train stations, while the chief of the National Police Agency, who was in charge of the Aum investigation, survived being shot four times as he entered the agency's headquarters.

To add to the drama, Hideo Murai, the chief scientist, was stabbed in front of TV cameras and died a few hours later. His killer was a Korean criminal with no known links to Aum, but many believed Aum had ordered the killing because he knew too much. Asahara and the some of the other leaders went into hiding. The police investigation proceeded with the painful slowness that had characterized all their dealings with Aum. They eventually arrested more than 150 Aum members, but initially no one was charged with crimes directly related to the subway gassing. As the public grew angrier, Aum's chief spokesperson, the boyish-looking Fumihiro Joyu, became an unlikely sex symbol for Japanese schoolgirls.

Asahara was finally arrested on 16 May. It seems that the Japanese police, who usually solve crimes by obtaining confessions, had been waiting to build a watertight case before moving in and making an arrest. He was found hiding in a compartment at the Mount Fuji complex, and had obviously been in there for quite some time. As police led the filthy, malodorous guru away, he said, 'Don't touch me. I don't even let my disciples touch me.'

The marathon Aum trials began in 1996. Asahara, represented by twelve lawyers, pleaded not guilty to twenty-three counts of murder. He refused to speak throughout the trial, even to his lawyers. He was sentenced to death, with his final appeal against the sentence rejected on 15 September 2006. Eleven other Aum leaders were also sentenced to death. In August 2009 he was still awaiting execution.

Very few people in Aum knew that the subway attack was going to happen, and afterwards, many found it hard to believe that Aum was responsible. The Japanese government tried unsuccessfully to have the organization banned, and it continues to exist under the name Aleph, with over 1,000 members. While it has renounced violence, its existence is a continuing source of anxiety to the Japanese people.

Some have seen Aum as a peculiarly Japanese phenomenon, a twisted expression of the country's conformity and deference to authority, and of a morality based on avoiding shame rather than admitting guilt. In his book on the subway attack, *Underground*, novelist Haruki Murakami wrote:

The Aum 'phenomenon' disturbs precisely because it is not someone else's affair. It shows us a distorted image of ourselves in a manner which none of us could have foreseen.

There is certainly truth in this (although it doesn't account for the cult's huge success in Russia). Perhaps the most sobering aspect of Aum was the number of scientists and other supposedly rational people who flocked to it and were willing to carry out Asahara's mad schemes. The end of the world may be a terrifying concept for most people, but for some it is strangely appealing.

The

SILEN+ CUL+

The Movement for
the Restoration of the
Ten Commandments of God
(Founded c. 1989)

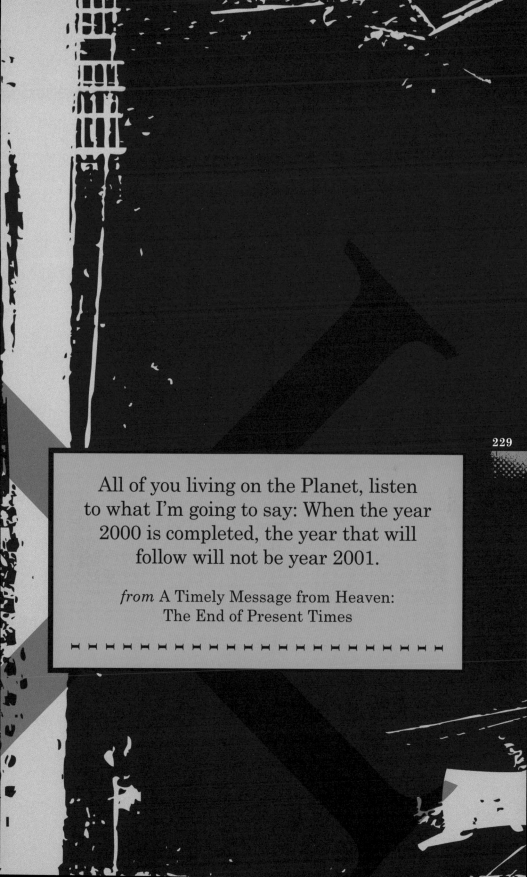

All of you living on the Planet, listen to what I'm going to say: When the year 2000 is completed, the year that will follow will not be year 2001.

from A Timely Message from Heaven: The End of Present Times

IT WAS A RELIGIOUS MOVEMENT LITTLE KNOWN EVEN IN ITS NATIVE UGANDA. Its members kept strictly to themselves, literally silent lest they inadvertently break the Ten Commandments. On the morning of 17 May 2000, 330 of them, including seventy-eight children, filed into a wooden church on their property in Kanungu. As they prayed inside, the windows were boarded up, the front door was locked, and the church was set on fire. Everyone inside it was incinerated.

At first, it seemed like another Jonestown-style mass suicide, and was reported as such around the world. Then the police began to dig up mass graves on other church properties, and an even more chilling scenario unfolded.

A LAND ⊕F VISI⊕NS

Uganda, a country blessed with a temperate climate and fertile land, has for decades been racked by wars, tribal conflicts and political repression. It has also been the breeding ground for hundreds of small religious movements, many of them apocalyptic in tone. About 80 percent of Ugandans are Christian (with half of those Roman Catholic) and these breakaway religious movements often mix Christianity with tribal beliefs. The most widely known outside the country is probably the Lord's Resistance Army. Led by a self-proclaimed spirit medium, Joseph Kony, the LRA became notorious during the 1990s for abducting children and forcing them to become soldiers. The goal of its war was supposedly the creation of a state run on the Ten Commandments.

With Catholicism so widespread in Uganda, it is not surprising that it has a tradition of religious visions, particularly of Jesus and the Virgin Mary. In the late 1980s, a woman named Gauda Kamushwa declared that she had seen the Virgin in a cave in Nyabugotam, in the western district of Rukungiri. Kamushwa gathered together a number of mainly female followers. A plump, middle-aged woman with a checkered past, Credonia Mwerinde, was one of them.

Mwerinde was born in the neighboring district of Kanungu in 1952. Her father, Paul Kashuku, who also claimed to have had visions, owned 10 acres of land near Kanungu town, a local trading center. Mwerinde dropped out of school early, had a number of children to different men and owned a bar, where she served banana beer brewed by her father. She was said by some to have been a prostitute, although it is possible she made this claim about herself to encourage comparisons with Mary Magdalene. Others have accused her of witchcraft, arson and even murder.

Mwerinde's bar went bust in mid-1988, and her ex-husband Eric Mazima has said that it was after this that she began to see visions of the Virgin Mary. While she was in Nyabugotam, she met a man named Joseph Kebwetere. Born in 1932, Kebwetere had been a schoolteacher, the founder and headmaster of a Catholic school, a public servant and a politician. He married a domestic science teacher named Teresa in 1960, and they had sixteen children. He was a wealthy man, respected in the community for his piety and charitable works. Softly spoken and introverted, he also suffered from bouts of depression that sometimes saw him hospitalized.

One day, Credonia Mwerinde, her sister Ursula and another woman approached Kebwetere. Mwerinde told him that she had received a message from the Virgin Mary instructing Kebwetere to take them in. Kebwetere agreed, and the three women went to live on his farm. They were eventually joined by some 200 others. Mwerinde spent most of her time shut in her room, writing out the messages she had received from the Virgin. In 1994, she and Kebwetere incorporated their group as a religion, the Movement for the Restoration of the Ten Commandments of God.

Teresa and her children eventually grew sick of all the strangers on their property—especially after Mwerinde set fire to all Teresa's clothes—and kicked them out. They went to Kanungu, where Mwerinde's dying father had donated his land to the Movement. Over the next few years, a self-sufficient community was created on this land, which was named 'Ishayuuriro rya Maria' ('the place where Mary rescues her people'). It included a church, a twenty-room house for the leaders, dormitories for ordinary members, a dairy farm, a cemetery and fields where potatoes, bananas and other crops were grown. A primary school operated for about a year until closed by the authorities because of unsanitary conditions and rumors that the children were being mistreated. (Given that the primary belief of the Movement was that the world was about to end, education was not a priority for them.) About 300 people lived in the Kanungu settlement at any given time, while there were about a dozen smaller camps in other parts of the country. Members were often moved between the camps.

The Movement was led by twelve apostles, half of them women. After Kebwetere and Mwerinde, the most important leader was a Catholic priest, Dominic Kataribabo, who had a Master's degree in religious studies from a Californian university. He became the Movement's 'bishop,' ordaining two other men as priests. They conducted its church services, which were essentially the same as regular Catholic services, although much longer. Members of the Movement were adamant that they had not broken away from the Catholic Church, although they said that it needed reform. Kebwetere, Kataribabo and several others were nevertheless excommunicated.

Most of the Movement's members were Catholics, although there were representatives of other religions as well. Members were predominately women and children (it was reported that many of them suffered from AIDS, but this was never confirmed). Very few people local to Kanungu joined, and it is suggested that Credonia Mwerinde's bad reputation in the area contributed to this.

While several of the leaders, including Kebwetere and Kataribabo, claimed to have visions, it was Mwerinde who was in daily contact with the Virgin Mary. No important decision was taken until she had been consulted. Mwerinde had so much control over people's daily lives that her nickname was 'the Programmer.'

On joining, a person was expected to donate all their money and possessions, including their clothing, to the Movement. All adults wore uniforms (black for novices, green and white for full members). Ordinary members followed a strictly regimented, monkish existence, with most hours of their day (which began at 3 a.m.) allotted to work or long periods of prayer. They survived on a meager diet, mainly posho (a porridge made from maize flour), beans, bananas and sweet potatoes, while Mondays, Wednesdays and Fridays were given over to fasting. Mortification of the flesh was encouraged, so they went barefoot and slept on the floor. (The lives of the leaders were considerably easier than this. The house they lived in was comfortable; they wore shoes and ate meat.) Sexual intercourse was strictly forbidden, and men and women slept in separate dormitories. Family members were separated and sent to different camps.

233

The most notable aspect of the Movement was the vow of silence. They communicated with each other using sign language, and on the rare occasions that an outsider visited the settlement, they wrote things down. The only time they were allowed to speak was when preaching to outsiders. The expressed aim of maintaining silence was to prevent members from breaking the eighth commandment, 'Thou shalt not bear false witness,' but it was also a powerful method of control. The order to be silent was said to have come from the Virgin Mary. It is not known which of the leaders received this message, but it bears the hallmarks of the retiring and introverted Kebwetere, who adhered strictly to the rule.

THE FAILED PROPHECY

The Movement's beliefs were set out in a book, *A Timely Message from Heaven: The End of Present Times*. New members were required to read it repeatedly, and it was said that anyone who read it twenty times would have all their prayers answered. The book contained transcriptions of messages from the Virgin Mary and set out the Movement's central belief, that the world would end on 31 December 2000, after darkness had covered Earth for three days. It was the task of members to prepare for this event through prayer, penance and self-mortification. The leaders compared their movement to an ark, and those who had fully accepted its teaching were said to be 'ready to die in the ark.' They would be the only people on Earth saved when the time came.

The prophecy's failure caused great consternation within the group. Discipline broke down. People stopped working and started speaking. Many demanded their money and property back. The leaders stalled. They said the Virgin Mary had told them the end of the world had been postponed, and when that failed to satisfy anyone, they announced a new date—17 May.

Those who continued to demand their money and property were told to put their complaints in writing. When their letters were received, they were called in for meetings with the leaders. After these meetings, they were usually not seen again by others in the group. People who asked about them were told they had gone to other camps.

The lead-up to 17 May saw frantic activity. The leaders sold off much of the church's property at rock-bottom prices, and settled accounts they had with local businesses. Members were sent out to talk to former members and urge them to be back at Kanungu for the appointed date. The daily work schedule was abandoned. The prayers and fasting continued, but at the same time, the ordinary members ate better than ever before. On the evening of 16 May, they had a huge feast. They ate the meat of their slaughtered cattle and drank Coca-Cola.

235

THE BURNING CHURCH

On the morning of 17 May, several hundred people gathered in the Kanungu settlement's new church, which was due to be officially opened the following day.

Sometime before 10 a.m., they left the new church and went into the old one. When they were inside, a man (possibly the farm manager, Robert Kanangura) was seen putting boards over the windows and nailing them shut. At about 10.30 a.m., the locals heard an explosion believed to have been caused by containers of gasoline placed inside the church. Those who came running to investigate could hear people screaming as it burned.

News of the slaughter quickly spread around the world. A mass suicide was assumed, and an erroneous report went out that those inside the church had doused themselves with paraffin before the fire. Then six bodies were found buried behind the leaders' house, in holes originally dug for latrines. The victims had been strangled or poisoned, and sulfuric acid had been poured on them in an attempt to decompose them.

Further discoveries over the next few days made the suicide scenario seem even less likely. One hundred and fifty-five bodies were found buried beneath or in the garden of Dominic Kataribabo's house in Rugazi (he had sold it to his nephew on 11 March). Two hundred and eighty-nine more bodies were found buried at three other Movement properties. Some of these victims had been strangled but most had been poisoned. The police eventually put the final death toll from the fire and related murders at 780.

These discoveries suggested that, with their prophecy a failure and members clamoring for their money (which had in all likelihood been spent), the leaders embarked on a killing spree. But this does not explain everything. Postmortems indicated that some of the bodies had been dead for up to a year, well before the prophecy failed.

The central mystery is the fate of the three leaders. The police initially announced they had identified one of the charred corpses in the church as Kataribabo, but later retracted this and issued warrants for his arrest, along with Kebwetere, Mwerinde and three others. Kebwetere's wife, Teresa, said that on the day before the fire, a parcel arrived at her home containing books, documents, and the church's certificate of registration. She said she believed her husband had died in the fire, but in 2001 told reporters that she had received information that he had actually died in June 1999 and was buried at Kataribabo's house in Rugazi. Police later said that they had found no evidence Kebwetere was seen by anyone in the six months before the fire.

One theory is that after Kebwetere died—possibly murdered by Mwerinde—there was an internal struggle within the leadership. Some members became disillusioned and threatened to leave, at which point the killings started. Then, when the prophecy failed and the cult was clearly falling apart, Mwerinde, Kataribabo and others decided to bring it to an end. Why they chose to do it in such an appalling way must remain a mystery, although Mwerinde's penchant for arson is suggestive. In such a scenario, it is highly unlikely that Mwerinde, Kataribabo and whoever else ordered the killings died in the fire. There is an unconfirmed report that Mwerinde was seen driving away from Kanungu in a pickup truck in the early hours of 17 May, accompanied by her sister, two children and a man. Another report has her leaving on a bus.

Other questions remain. Who carried out the murders? One suggestion made by the police was that the six bodies found buried behind the leaders' house were the remains of the men who had carried out killings for the leaders prior to the fire. After all, if they had not been discovered, the suicide theory would probably have been accepted by everyone, and the other mass graves would never have been found.

How were so many murders covered up? The Movement's secrecy, and the docility and habitual silence of its members, were certainly key factors here, yet the sheer number of killings, carried out in the most populous region of Uganda, remains staggering. And where did the survivors go? Most accounts of the Movement estimate its total membership as 4,000 or higher. There is a grim possibility that further mass graves exist which the police did not have the resources to find.

237

BIBLIOGRAPHY

General books on cults and new religious movements

Bromley, David G. and Anson D. Shupe, *Strange Gods: the Great American Cult Scare*, Beacon Books, Boston, 1981.

Lewis, James A., *The Encyclopedia of Cults, Sects and New Religions*, Prometheus Books, New York, 1998.

Melton, J. Gordon, *Encyclopedic Handbook of Cults in America*, Garland, New York, 1992.

Ritchie, Jean, *The Secret World of Cults*, Angus & Robertson, London, 1991.

Scheflin, Alan W., and Edward M. Opton, Jr, *The Mind Manipulators*, Paddington Press, New York, 1978.

Shupe, Anson D. (ed), *Wolves Within the Fold: Religious Leadership and Abuses of Power*, Rutgers University Press, New Brunswick, 1998.

Tucker, Ruth A., *Another Gospel*, Academic Books, Grand Rapids, 1989.

Web pages

CESNUR (Center for Studies of New Religions) – www.cesnur.org

Cultic Studies Review – http://cultsandsociety.com/Default.htm

The Religious Movements Homepage Project @The University of Virginia – http://religiousmovements.lib.virginia.edu/home.htm

The Rick A. Ross Institute for the Study of Destructive Cults, Controversial Groups and Movements – www.rickross.com

Thuggee

Dash, Mike, *Thug: the True Story of India's Murderous Cult*, Granta Books, London, 2005.

Larsen, Egon, *Strange Sects and Cults*, Arthur Barker, London, 1971.

Sleeman, James L., *Thug, or A Million Murders*, Pilgrims, Delhi, 1998.

Serpent Handlers/The Church of God With Signs Following

Covington, Dennis, *Salvation on Sand Mountain*, Penguin, New York, 1996.

Faulk, Kent, 'Snake Kills Evangelist,' *The Birmingham News*, 6 October 1998.

Kimbrough, David, *Taking Up Serpents*, Mercer University Press, Macon, 2002.

La Barre, Weston, *They Shall Take Up Serpents*, Schocken Books, New York, 1969.

The Branch Davidians
Boyer, Peter J., 'Burned,' *The New Yorker*, 1 November 1999.
Gibbs, Nancy, 'Tragedy in Waco', *Time*, 3 May 1993.
Lewis, James R. (ed), *From the Ashes: Making Sense of Waco*, Rowman & Littlefield, Lanham, 1994.
McCarthy, Phillip, 'Apocalypse vow,' *The Sydney Morning Herald*, 12 April 1993.
Reavis, Dick J., *The Ashes of Waco*, Syracuse University Press, 1998.
Steinke, Darcey, 'God Rocks,' *Spin*, 1993.

Mankind United/Christ's Church of the Golden Rule
Anonymous, 'Profit's Prophet,' *Time*, 21 May 1945.
Anonymous (Arthur Bell), *Mankind United, a Challenge to "Mad Ambition" and "The Money Changers" accompanied by an Invitation to the World's "Sane" Men and Women*, The International Registration Bureau (Pacific Coast Division of North America), n.p., 1938.
Dohrman, H.T., *California Cult*, Beacon Press, Boston, 1958.
Stephenson, Denice, *Dear People: Remembering Jonestown*, Heyday Books, Berkeley, 1905.

Peoples Temple
Chester, David, *Salvation and Suicide*, Indiana University Press, Bloomington, 1988.
Mills, Jeannie, *Six Years with God*, A.W. Publishers, New York, 1979.
Reiterman, Tim, *Raven: the Untold Story of Jim Jones and his People*, Dutton, New York, 1982.

Synanon
Janzen, Rod, *The Rise and Fall of Synanon*, Johns Hopkins University Press, Baltimore, 2001.
Mitchell, Dave, Cathy Mitchell and Richard Ofshe, *The Light on Synanon*, Seaview Books, n.p., 1980.

Rajneeshism
Cater, Nick, 'Virtual words of wisdom from a guru in a beanie,' *The Sunday Telegraph*, 30 July 1995.
Gordon, James S., *The Golden Guru*, The Stephen Greene Press, Lexington, 1987.
Guilliatt, Richard, 'It was a time of madness,' *The Weekend Australian Magazine*, 17–18 June 2006.
Hamilton, Rosemary, *Hellbent for Enlightenment*, White Cloud Press, Ashland, 1998.
Wright, Charles, *Oranges and Lemmings*, Greenhouse Publications, Melbourne, 1985.

The Manson Family
Atkins, Susan, with Bob Slosser, *Child of Satan, Child of God*, Hodder & Stoughton, Kent, 1978.

Bugliosi, Vincent and Curt Gentry, *Helter Skelter*, Penguin, London, 1982.

Sanders, Ed, *The Family*, Rupert Hart-Davis, London, 1972.

Schreck, Nikolas (ed), *The Manson File*, Amok Press, New York, 1988.

Watkins, Paul, with Guillermo Soleded, *My Life with Charles Manson*, Bantam, New York, 1979.

The Church of the Lamb of God

Bradlee, Ben, and Dale Van Atta, *Prophet of Blood*, Putnam, New York, 1981.

Chynoweth, Rena with Dean M. Shapiro, *The Blood Covenant*, Diamond Books, Austin, 1990.

LeBaron, Verlan, *The LeBaron Story*, Keels & Co, Lubbock, 1981.

MOVE

Bowser, Charles W., *Let the Bunker Burn*, Camino Books, Philadelphia, 1989.

Anderson, John, and Hilary Hevenor, *Burning Down the House*, Norton, New York, 1987.

Heaven's Gate

Gleick, Elizabeth, 'The Marker We've Been Waiting For,' *Time*, 7 April 1997.

Kossy, Donna, *Strange Creations*, Feral House, Los Angeles, 2001.

Perkins, Rodney, and Forrest Jackson, *Cosmic Suicide*, Pentadial Press, Dallas, 1997.

Vallee, Jacques, *Messengers of Deception*, And/Or Press, Berkeley, 1979.

The Ant Hill Kids

'Canadian cult leader Theriault denied parole,' Canadian Press, 11 July 2002.

Kaihla, Paul and Ross Laver, *Savage Messiah*, Doubleday, Toronto, 1993.

Nation of Yahweh

Freedberg, Sydney P., *Brother Love*, Pantheon, New York, 1994.

Martin, Douglas, 'Yahweh ben Yahweh, Leader of Separatist Sect, Dies at 71,' *The New York Times*, 9 May 2007.

Jeffery Lundgren and the Kirtland Cult

Earley, Pete, *Prophet of Death*, Avon, New York, 1991.

Sassé, Cynthia Stalter and Peggy Murphy Widder, *The Kirtland Massacre*, Zebra Books, New York, 1991.

The Order of the Solar Temple

Allison, Col, Duncan Graham and Tony Grant-Taylor, 'Doomsday down under,' *The Sydney Morning Herald*, 15 October 1994.

'Death of a Cult,' *The Weekend Australian*, 15-16 October 1994.

Lewis, James R. (ed), *The Order of the Solar Temple*, Ashgate, Aldershot, 2006.

Aum Shinrikyo

Green, Shane, 'Asahara's lack of remorse adds to the pain,'
The Weekend Australian, 26–27 April 2003.

Kaplan, David E., and Andrew Marshall, *The Cult at the End of the World*, Arrow, London, 1996.

Marshall, Andrew, 'Return of the killer cult,' *The Good Weekend*, 17 July 1999.

Mitchell, Michael, 'Sect pulls out all the stops to survive,'
The Sydney Morning Herald, 22 January 2000.

Murakami, Haruki, *Underground*, Vintage, London, 2003.

Robinson, Gwen, 'Cult of insanity,' *The Weekend Australian*, 20–21 May 1995.

The Movement for the Restoration of the Ten Commandments of God

'After the world's end,' *The Sydney Morning Herald*, 31 March 2000.

Eichstaedt, Peter, 'Uganda: Ghoulish Plan for Cult Killing Site,'
Institute for War and Peace, 3 May 2006.

Kabazzi-Kisirinya, S., Nkurunziza R.K. Deusdedit and Gerard Banura (eds), *The Kanungu Cult-Saga: Suicide, Murder or Salvation?*, Department of Religious Studies, Makarere University, Makarere, 2000.

Majumi, James, 'Kebwetere Died in 1999,' *New Vision*, 19 May 2001.

Mugisha, Matthias, 'Kunungu Dead Poisoned,' *New Vision*, 28 July 2000.

Santoro, Lara, 'Priestess of Death,' *Newsweek International*, 6 August 2000.

241

ACKNOWLEDGMENTS

Every reasonable effort has been made to trace the owners of copyright materials in this book, but is some instances this has proven impossible. The author and publisher will be glad to receive information leading to more complete acknowledgments in subsequent printings of the book and in the meantime extend their apologies for any omissions.

Page 119: Reprinted by permission of SLL/Sterling Lord Literistic, Inc. Copyright by Benjamin C. Bradlee.

Page 161: Excerpted from *Savage Messiah: The Shocking Story of Cult Leader Rock Thériault and the Women Who Loved Him* by Paul Kaihla and Ross Laver. Copyright © 1993 Paul Kaihla and Ross Laver. Reprinted by permission of Doubleday Canada.

Page 201: © 'The Order of the Solar Temple: The Temple of Death,' by James R Lewis, 2006, Ashgate.

INDEX

G

Gaines, Linda 177, 178, 181, 182, 186
Gandhi, Mahatma 93
Garretson, William 113
Genoud, Gerry and Collette 208, 210
Giacobino, Albert 209
Giguère, Jacques 164–8, 172
Glassey, Donald 137, 139–40, 141
gnosticism 159
Golden Way (Geneva) 203–4
Goode, Wilson 136, 142–6
Grand-Maison, Jocelyne 206
Green, Aston 180, 183
Grenier, Francine 162
Grenier, Maryse 164–9
Grenier, Miriam 169
Grenier, Samuel 166–7
Grogan, 'Clem' 114
Gurdjieff, G. I. 93

H

Halhed, Nathaniel 17
Hamilton, Rosemary 94–5
Harden, Tom 30–1
Hare Krishnas 7
Hayakawa, Kiyohide 220
Hayes, Raymond 30
Heaven's Gate 150–9
Helter Skelter (race war) 106, 111–15, 116
'Helter Skelter' (song) 111–12
Hensley, George Went 28–9, 30–1, 34
Hinduism 18, 23, 24–5, 221
Hinman, Bobby 107
Hinman, Gary 110–11
Hossyn, Gholam 16
Houteff, Florence 41
Houteff, Victor 40
Howell, Vernon 10, 42–51
Hughes, Anna 43, 44
Hughes, Ronald 117
Hunter, Edward 8

I

India 16–25, 96
International Chivalric Organization of the Solar Tradition 204 *see also* Order of the Solar Temple
International Institute of Universal Research and Administration 54–6, 57 *see also* Mankind United
International Legion of Vigilantes 59
Israel, Branch Davidians in 41, 42

J

Jain, Chandra Mohan 92
Jainism 92
James, William 102
Japan 7, 214, 215, 218–19, 224–6
Jensen, Kristina 123
John Africa 136–44, 147
Johnson, Benjamin 121–2
Johnson, Keith and Kathy 197–9
Jone, Father (Billy Jones) 177
Jones, Reverend Jim 10, 66–77
Jones, Lynetta 66, 67
Jones, Marceline 67, 73
Jones, Rachel 42
Jones, Stephan Gandhi 68, 73, 77
Jonestown (Guyana) 8, 50, 70, 71, 72–7
Jordan, Dan 124–5, 126, 132
Jouret, Luc 203–11
Jouret, Marie-Christine 203–4, 211
Joyu, Fumihiro 225
Judaism 178

K

Kamushwa, Gauda 230–1
Kanangura, Robert 235
Karpis, Alvin 108
Kasabian, Linda 113, 116

Project Manager: Paul O'Beirne
Editor: Janine Flew
Design: Hugh Ford

Metro Books
122 Fifth Avenue
New York, NY 10011

ISBN-13: 978-1-4351-2257-4

Printed and bound in China

1 3 5 7 9 10 8 6 4 2